Sex in the Bible

Sex in the Bible

THE UNTOLD TRUTH

Evan P. Turner

No part of this publication may be reproduced, stored in a retrieval system, or transmitted, in any form or by any means—electronic, mechanical, photocopying, recording, or otherwise—without the written prior permission of the author.

Unless stated otherwise, all quotes from scripture are from the King James Version.

Copyright © 2015 Evan P. Turner
All rights reserved.

ISBN: 1512255645
ISBN 13: 9781512255645

Library of Congress Control Number: 2015914928
CreateSpace Independent Publishing Platform
North Charleston, SC

Contents

Introduction 1
Chapter 1 Covetousness/Lust/Desire, Masturbation, and Nudity 17
Chapter 2 Adultery, Polygyny, and Divorce 35
Chapter 3 Divorce + Remarriage = Adultery 55
Chapter 4 Sex Outside of Wedlock and Rape 83
Chapter 5 Anal Sex 143
Chapter 6 Menstruation 161
Chapter 7 Incest, Bestiality and Customs 167
Chapter 8 Sex in Heaven 173

Introduction

To understand sexual sins, we need to understand the exact meaning of sin. Now, most Christians believe sin is the transgression or violation of God's law, as 1 John 3:4 states: "Whoever commits sin transgresses also the law: for sin is the transgression of the law." But when interpreting the Bible, we must compare scripture with scripture, and this verse conflicts with Hebrews 9:22, which says that "almost all things are by the law purged with blood; and without shedding of blood is no remission." God commanded man in the Garden of Eden and after the great Flood to be fruitful and multiply (Gen. 1:22; 28; 9:1). Yet no one says that being a virgin or not having any children is a sin against God.

However, this doesn't change the fact that anyone who isn't being fruitful and multiplying is transgressing the law; this is a direct command from God—one that has not been repealed. Nobody regards such a violation as a sin, even if this squarely contradicts 1 John 3:4. The very fact that nobody dares question singleness or childlessness should be sufficient evidence that a more nuanced definition of sin is required. By employing a much more consistent method of comparing scripture with scripture, we can deduce a simple yet consistent way of defining sin.

When we compare 1 John 3:4 with Hebrews 9:22, at first the two appear to contradict each other, but this isn't the case. On closer examination, the two verses go quite well together. The author of Hebrews stated that almost all sins required the shedding of blood, so we can logically conclude that some sins didn't require the shedding of blood. Comparing scripture with scripture is always important because in many cases certain laws are qualified. One example is vows. Jesus stated in Matthew 5:33–37,

> Again, ye have heard that it hath been said by them of old time, Thou shalt not forswear thyself, but shalt perform unto the Lord thine oaths: But I say unto you, Swear not at all; neither by heaven; for it is God's throne: Nor by the earth; for it is his footstool: neither by Jerusalem; for it is the city of the great King. Neither shalt thou swear by thy head, because thou canst not make one hair white or black. But let your communication be, Yea, yea; Nay, nay: for whatsoever is more than these cometh of evil.

At least on the surface, Jesus seemingly forbade all oaths, swearing, or vows. But is this actually the case? Let's now compare Jesus's seeming rejection of vows with a vow that can be construed to contradict his previous statements. Matthew 19:9 says, "And I say unto you, Whosoever shall put away his wife, except it be for fornication, and shall marry another, committeth adultery: and whoso marrieth her which is put away doth commit adultery."

Apparently, in this instance, Jesus actually upheld vows. Who would deny that a marriage vow is a solemn promise to perform an activity? If this wasn't the case, then why did he state that marrying a divorced woman was adultery? This can only be due to the fact that God still recognizes the vows she made to her first husband. Some Christians foolishly employ Pharisee-type tactics and say marriage isn't a vow but simply a covenant, but there is no difference between the two; however, this foolhardy approach to scripture is no different from that of the Pharisees, who believed they could violate their vows by swearing by anyone or thing other than God.

This brings us to our next point in Matthew 5:34–37. Jesus stated that we're not to make a vow by heaven, earth, or even our own heads; according to the Pharisees, by making such vows and not abiding by them, they weren't sinning against God. In fact, Jesus wasn't forbidding vows per se

Introduction

but simply pointing out that one shouldn't make vows with loopholes; if one does, he or she would still be sinning against God. Rather than swearing by heaven or earth, simply state what it is you plan to do; this in no way negates a vow, as many Christians have come to mistakenly believe. If you told a friend you'd pick him up at the airport at 5:00 p.m., you've made a vow to him; it's as simple as that. Jesus did not say you cannot make a vow; rather, he spoke against supposed loopholes people used not to fulfill their vows.

God gave to Israel regulations concerning vows in Numbers 30:1–16; Jesus just clarified the Pharisees' misapplication. Besides, Jesus himself made a vow: "But I say unto you, I won't drink henceforth of this fruit of the vine, until that day when I drink it new with you in my Father's kingdom" (Matt. 26:29). When one fails to study scripture in detail, many problems are sure to spring forth. Indeed, this mistake breeds contradiction. A meticulous study of scripture, on the other hand, harmonizes Jesus's words with those of God and other believers. Acts 18:18 says, "And Paul after this tarried there yet a good while, and then took his leave of the brethren, and sailed thence into Syria, and with him Priscilla and Aquila; having shorn his head in Cenchrea: for he had a vow." Paul is proof that Christians were still making vows after Jesus ascended to heaven.

When you study scripture and compare it with other scripture, you get a much clearer view of scripture, and supposed contradictions disappear. So we see that Jesus didn't nullify God's laws concerning vows; rather, he upheld them by stating that one shouldn't vow by heaven or one's head. This in no way means Christians cannot make vows to other people or to God; it means only that our yes should mean yes. Jesus's words are qualified through his other statements regarding vows and with God's laws mentioned in the Old Testament. "But wait," you might say, "we aren't under the law anymore." We will address this point shortly; until then we need to continue seeking out a consistent method of defining sin.

Let's return to God's command to be fruitful and multiply. We should note that God never penalized anyone for not having children, and there were many godly men and women in the Bible who didn't have children, including his only begotten Son, Jesus. Thus, we can logically conclude that 1 John 3:4, which states that any transgression of God's law is sin, is in fact a qualified statement much like Jesus's statement in regard to vows. As mentioned earlier, we can use Hebrews 9:22 to qualify 1 John 3:4, and we can conclude that one who isn't fruitful and doesn't multiply isn't sinning, because at no time did not having children require the shedding of blood. Let's go over more of God's laws and determine whether breaking these commands is sin.

Deuteronomy 22:10 states, "Thou shalt not plow with an ox and an ass together." Interestingly enough, few, if any, Christians believe that any Israelite who plowed his or her field with an ox yoked with an ass was sinning against God, despite the fact that 1 John 3:4 would define such an act as a sin against God. By using Hebrews 9:22 to qualify 1 John 3:4, we can once again safely conclude that yoking an ox with an ass is by no means a sin. Are you confused, or do you have doubts? This law had a higher spiritual meaning in 1 Corinthians 7:12–16, where Paul told believers not to depart from unbelievers:

> But to the rest speak I, not the Lord: If any brother hath a wife that believeth not, and she be pleased to dwell with him, let him not put her away. And the woman which hath an husband that believeth not, and if he be pleased to dwell with her, let her not leave him. For the unbelieving husband is sanctified by the wife, and the unbelieving wife is sanctified by the husband: else were your children unclean; but now are they holy. But if the unbelieving depart, let him depart. A brother or a sister is not under bondage in such cases: but God hath called us to peace. For what knowest thou, O wife, whether thou shalt save thy husband? or how knowest thou, O man, whether thou shalt save thy wife?

If being unequally yoked was a sin, Paul wouldn't have been able to say this. Combine the fact that there was no shedding of blood for having two different animals yoked together, and understand that most of ancient Israel's

Introduction

laws were a shadow of higher spiritual meaning. Here we find the meaning in 2 Corinthians 6:14, where Paul said we shouldn't be unequally yoked with unbelievers. "Be ye not unequally yoked together with unbelievers: for what fellowship hath righteousness with unrighteousness? and what communion hath light with darkness?" Obviously, if a Christian marries a non-Christian, they are going to have a hard time living together in a relationship; in a similar way, it's unwise, to say the least, to yoke an ox with an ass.

People might look at the concept of being unequally yoked as odd or weird, much like a farmer plowing a field with an ox yoked with an ass, but it's not a sin. Otherwise, Paul would have contradicted himself in 1 Corinthians 7:12–16. The point most Christians miss is that it's not a sin to be unequally yoked; this is what God said in Deuteronomy 22:10 and Paul said in 1 Corinthians 7:12–16.

Moving on to another of God's laws he gave to Israel, let us turn to Leviticus 19:17–18.

> Thou shalt not hate thy brother in thine heart: thou shalt in any wise rebuke thy neighbour, and not suffer sin upon him. Thou shalt not avenge, nor bear any grudge against the children of thy people, but thou shalt love thy neighbour as thyself: I am the Lord.

We now come across another law that didn't require the shedding of blood, which again explains the "almost" of Hebrews 9:22. It would appear—on the surface at least—that we are in a quandary. If we simply appeal to 1 John 3:4 to state that hating our brother or neighbor is sin, then it would be foolish or hypocritical to say that yoking an ox with an ass isn't a sin; it's clearly forbidden even though it didn't require the shedding of blood, it also wasn't required for actually hating somebody. We're now in the "cherry-picking" trap; if we simply stick with 1 John 3:4 to conveniently condemn hate as a sin while at the same time using Hebrews 9:22 to state that yoking to different kinds of animals or not growing a beard isn't a sin, then we're simply illogical.

We must find a way to qualify both 1 John 3:4 and Hebrews 9:22 so they harmonize with the rest of scripture. The gift of the Spirit was given at Pentecost, and God's law is now written in the heart of believers, as Jeremiah 31:33–34 states:

> But this shall be the covenant that I will make with the house of Israel; After those days, saith the Lord, I will put my law in their inward parts, and write it in their hearts; and will be their God, and they shall be my people. And they shall teach no more every man his neighbour, and every man his brother, saying, Know the Lord: for they shall all know me, from the least of them unto the greatest of them, saith the Lord: for I will forgive their iniquity, and I will remember their sin no more.

So in addition to God's law, proclaimed at Mount Sinai, we have the gift of the Spirit, and with this gift comes fruit, as Jesus tells us in Matthew 7:16–20.

> Ye shall know them by their fruits. Do men gather grapes of thorns, or figs of thistles? Even so every good tree bringeth forth good fruit; but a corrupt tree bringeth forth evil fruit. A good tree cannot bring forth evil fruit, neither can a corrupt tree bring forth good fruit. Every tree that bringeth not forth good fruit is hewn down, and cast into the fire. Wherefore by their fruits ye shall know them.

We have a certain qualifier for 1 John 3:4 and Hebrews 9:22; we are to know believers by their fruit. We must search the scriptures to see whether we can know the details of the fruit Christians should bear. Paul told us in Galatians 5:22–23 what the exact fruit of the Spirit is: "But the fruit of the Spirit is love, joy, peace, longsuffering, gentleness, goodness, faith, Meekness, temperance: against such there is no law."

Using Paul's detailed description of the fruit of the Spirit along with Jesus's words that we are known by our fruit, we can now use the fruit of

Introduction

the Spirit as a qualifier for 1 John 3:4 and Hebrews 9:22. Armed with this knowledge of scripture, we can now state with confidence that believers are expected to exhibit fruit of the Spirit and that violating any of these nine traits is a sin against God. We can conclude that while hating someone didn't require the shedding of blood, no one can deny that it is in violation of the fruit of the Spirit; thus, we can say that no believer should hate anybody. We can also state that while believers are required to produce the fruit of the Spirit, this doesn't mean unbelievers aren't sinning when they hate their neighbor. Such a conclusion would make no sense given that God gave the law to Israel while simultaneously condemning the heathen (pagan) nations, even though they hadn't been given (nor were they aware of) any of his laws.

We have to ask ourselves whether there are any more definitions of sin, in addition to the previous two we've already covered. The answer is yes, there are. Sin is mentioned in Ephesians 5–6.

> Wives, submit yourselves unto your own husbands, as unto the Lord. For the husband is the head of the wife, even as Christ is the head of the church: and he is the saviour of the body. Therefore as the church is subject unto Christ, so let the wives be to their own husbands in every thing. (Eph. 5:22–24)

> Children, obey your parents in the Lord: for this is right. Honour thy father and mother; (which is the first commandment with promise;) That it may be well with thee, and thou mayest live long on the earth. (Eph. 6:1–3)

We find that the definition of sin also includes the disobedience of wives to their husbands and the disobedience of children to their parents. By comparing scripture with scripture, we can piece together a fuller and more consistent picture of God's Word and his laws, and we can summarize as follows: "Whosoever committeth sin transgresseth also the law: for sin is the transgression of the law" (1 John 3:4). Whenever the following criteria are met, sin has occurred.

1. Something is a sin if it required the shedding of blood.
2. Something is a sin if it violates any of the nine fruit of the Spirit.
3. Something is a sin if in it one disobeys the family hierarchy (husbands, wives, and children).
4. Something is a sin if the intent is to break a law that meets any of the three previous criteria.

This definition of sin is much more consistent and simpler than any other method that tries to define what sin is. Even if the reader disregards or disagrees with the definition given here, he or she must admit that the typical answer of 1 John 3:4 is insufficient as the sole reply to inquirers. It also leads the purveyor of such doctrine to be criticized of cherry-picking the violation of certain laws while ignoring others.

With these pieces in place, the picture of God's law becomes clearer. Take, for instance, the cleanliness laws God gave Israel to separate them from the other nations. When God gave the list of unclean animals to eat, he said in Leviticus 11:31–35 that anyone who touched them would bathe in water and be unclean until the evening (night). Any vessel or sack had to be bathed in water, and any earthen vessel had to be broken. If anyone went to the temple unclean, he or she would be struck dead (Lev. 17:16). It should be noted, however, that this wasn't because the person touched or ate something unclean but because he or she disobeyed God and went to the sanctuary unclean. Those Christians who insist the cleanliness laws must still be kept and that eating pork is sin because it is unclean are silent regarding the following. Leviticus 15:16–18 says,

> And if any man's seed of copulation go out from him, then he shall wash all his flesh in water, and be unclean until the even. And every garment, and every skin, whereon is the seed of copulation, shall be washed with water, and be unclean until the even. The woman also with whom man shall lie with seed of copulation, they shall both bathe themselves in water, and be unclean until the even.

Introduction

The fact is that a couple who had sex in ancient Israel were considered unclean, not unlike someone who touched or even ate an unclean animal. It's interesting (isn't it?) that people who uphold the unclean/clean food dichotomy are completely silent on this issue, as they are with numerous other areas that resulted in rendering someone unclean. Let us return to the couple who had sex. Let's say they went to the temple despite God's command not to; they would have been struck dead. Simply put, their deaths would be due to the fact that they disobeyed God and went to the temple unclean. Having sex isn't in itself sinful, provided the couple didn't break any of God's laws related to sex; likewise, someone who touched or ate an animal wasn't sinning but was unclean only for a time. Going to the temple unclean would have been sin—this was the issue that would have concerned the Israelites.

There's nothing wrong with choosing to follow cleanliness laws, but anyone who teaches that these laws must be kept is clearly in the wrong. The cleanliness laws were only in relation to the temple and to keep Israel separate from other nations. "Thus shall you separate the children of Israel from their uncleanness; that they die not in their uncleanness, when they defile my tabernacle that is among them" (Lev. 15:31–33). As Paul stated, the scripture teaches we are now God's temple: "God that made the world and all things therein, seeing that he is Lord of heaven and earth, dwells not in temples made with hands" (Acts 17:24). God ripped the veil at the death of Christ, signifying that his presence left the temple (Matt. 27:51). We should also note that there's absolutely zero scriptural evidence to support the belief that eating bacon is sin but that eating from a plate at a restaurant or house that had made contact with unclean meat is not. Why are these same people who uphold the cleanliness laws not concerned with touching a menstruating woman? Or anything she might have made contact with (Lev. 15:19–24)? Excuses such as "Well, I try my best" or "We all sin" are simply cop-outs. Of course, if they were to admit that they don't worry about touching a menstruating woman or eating off a "defiled" plate because God no longer dwells in temples made with hands, they would be correct. However, they would also be defeating their own argument because cleanliness laws were related only to the temple, and this would include the laws related to unclean meat.

Looking further in Leviticus (5:2–3), we find the following:

> Or if a soul touch any unclean thing, whether it be a carcase of an unclean beast, or a carcase of unclean cattle, or the carcase of unclean creeping things, and if it be hidden from him; he also shall be unclean, and guilty. Or if he touch the uncleanness of man, whatsoever uncleanness it be that a man shall be defiled withal, and it be hid from him; when he knoweth of it, then he shall be guilty.

The shedding of blood was required only if someone who became unclean forgot to cleanse himself or herself; it was never required if someone cleansed himself or herself after moving an animal carcass or eating shrimp, for that matter. It was never evil to touch the deceased or to eat lobster, despite what some people will tell you. It is impossible to hold that a married couple who had sex weren't unclean while simultaneously stating that eating shellfish was sin. Do those who insist dietary laws must still be maintained believe Elijah sinned in the book of 1 Kings (17:4–7)?

> And it shall be, that thou shalt drink of the brook; and I have commanded the ravens to feed thee there. So he went and did according unto the word of the Lord: for he went and dwelt by the brook Cherith, that is before Jordan. And the ravens brought him bread and flesh in the morning, and bread and flesh in the evening; and he drank of the brook. And it came to pass after a while, that the brook dried up, because there had been no rain in the land.

In closing, the laws related to what was clean or unclean aren't unlike a mother telling her son, who was playing outside, to wash his hands before eating—but the child refuses to wash his hands. So the child is punished—not because he played outside but because he disobeyed her command to wash his hands. Unfortunately, some confuse God's

Introduction

commands to cleanse oneself after being unclean with doing an action that results in being unclean.

We return to the main purpose of this tome with a question. What are sexual sins according to the Word of God? When someone asks such a question, the usual answer is "Flee fornication. Every sin that a man doeth is without the body; but he that committeth fornication sinneth against his own body" (1 Cor. 6:18).

Many Christians mistakenly believe the preceding verse answers the question, but in reality it only begs the question. What exactly is "fornication" or, as other translations say, "harlotry," "prostitution," "sexual immorality," and so forth? To find the answer, we must compare scripture with scripture and determine whether there are any qualifications to Paul's statement. Thus far, we've discovered that sin is defined not by 1 John 3:4 but by several other criteria; similarly, we will find that several other criteria define sexual sins.

First, we must realize what Paul meant when he spoke of "fornication," which is translated from the Greek word *porneia*. It is now time to address the permanence of God's laws and tackle one of the biggest misconceptions of Christianity, which is Jesus's words concerning God's law. By misinterpreting Jesus's Sermon on the Mount, Christians have inadvertently caused an avalanche of misconceptions that have inevitably snowballed into what makes many err in their walk with God. Matthew 5:17–19 says,

> Think not that I am come to destroy the law, or the prophets: I am not come to destroy, but to fulfil. For verily I say unto you, Till heaven and earth pass, one jot or one tittle shall in no wise pass from the law, till all be fulfilled. Whosoever therefore shall break one of these least commandments, and shall teach men so, he shall be called the least in the kingdom of heaven: but whosoever shall do and teach them, the same shall be called great in the kingdom of heaven.

The traditional interpretation of Jesus's word states that he abolished God's law and introduced new laws, which are much stricter than the laws God gave at Mount Sinai. However, on closer examination this long-held view presents three problems. First, Jesus plainly said that he had not come to abolish the law but to fulfill it; yet, the traditional view holds that "fulfill" means "abolished," which leads to Jesus's saying the following nonsensical statement: "I did not come to abolish the law, but I came to abolish the law."

The author is aware of the semantic sleight of hand some employ by stating "fulfill" doesn't mean "abolish" but "nullify," "abrogate," or "replace." It doesn't really matter that all these words still lead to a nonsensical outcome of Jesus's doing away with the law while simultaneously claiming he didn't come to destroy it.

Second, Jesus said,

Whosoever therefore shall break one of these least commandments,
and shall teach men so, he shall be called the least in the kingdom
of heaven: but whosoever shall do and teach them, the same
shall be called great in the kingdom of heaven. (Matt. 5:19)

So, according to the traditional view, Jesus, who they believe abolished the law, is the least in the kingdom of heaven because he did away with the law.

Third, Jesus said, "Till heaven and earth pass, one jot or one tittle shall in no wise pass from the law, till all be fulfilled" (Matt. 5:18). We can all agree that heaven and earth haven't passed away since Jesus's ascension; therefore, we can safely conclude that God's law hasn't passed away.

When one understands that the Greek word for "fulfill," which is *pleroo*, is defined as "complete or render full," Jesus's words now make sense. Jesus didn't come to abolish or destroy the law but to render it full or to complete the law. In other words, he came to obey the law. This is an important point because all Christians agree that Jesus is our high priest, as the author of Hebrews (4:14) tells us; in fact, the entire point of the letter to the Hebrews is to tell us that the Levitical priesthood has been superseded. This also includes animal sacrifices and the need for a physical temple; yet many Christians, in their zeal to upend God's law based on

Introduction

an erroneous interpretation of Matthew 5:17–19, miss the significance of Hebrews. When one believes in the wholesale destruction of God's law, there is no opportunity to notice its many nuances. This thinking always leads to innumerable problems and inconsistencies.

Because we've already learned how to scripturally define sin, there's no need to answer such questions as "What about mixed fabrics?" and the like. Now it's just a matter of going through scripture to identify God's laws in regard to sex and to compare scripture with scripture to ensure such laws are, or are not, qualified. It will become plainly obvious, sometimes painfully so, that during our study of scripture, the traditional interpretation of Matthew 5:17–19 presents all types of contradictions and problems in relation to God's view of sex.

Besides, the traditional interpretation begs the following question: How can there be any laws against sex if Jesus abolished the law? If Jesus replaced the law given at Mount Sinai with a more stringent set, where did he call anal sex a sin? For those who say Paul did, how can you explain where he got this prohibition? He either made it up by himself or got it from God's law, which was given to Israel through the prophet Moses; Jesus wasn't recorded making such a prohibition. What is the most logical answer?

Let's return to Paul's oft-quoted statement in 1 Corinthians 6:18 about *porneia* being translated as "fornication." Most Christians get their definition of words from modern dictionaries instead of from comparing scripture with scripture. As a result, Christians have stated that a variety of actions qualify as "fornication" or "sexual immorality," from masturbation to sex outside of wedlock and so forth. The belief that Jesus has abolished God's law has led to a free-for-all in terms of what is sinful and what isn't. Unfortunately, many Bible dictionaries have fallen into the same trap, leading many Christians to simply pick up a *Strong's Concordance* and say unmarried sex is fornication, which Paul condemned repeatedly. Therefore, for a couple to engage in such an activity is forbidden.

This is nothing more than eisegesis, which is reading one's own ideas into scripture. Hardly does anyone ever start from the Old Testament and work his or her way to the New Testament; rather, people work backward and use the New Testament to interpret the Old Testament. By properly using the Old Testament to interpret the New Testament and arming oneself with the scriptural definition of sin, we can make the following preliminary conclusions, all of which we will address in more detail later. God's law in relation to masturbation and nudity will be studied in detail. Adultery (which includes remarriage after divorce), incest, bestiality, anal sex, sex during menstruation, and rape will be analyzed. God's law mentions sexual idolatry (also known as sacred prostitution)—that is, sex as a form of worship to a god. We will examine this concept along with rape, lust, and covetousness. The term "polygyny," which is defined as one man married to multiple women, will be used rather than the more broad term "polygamy," and so will the term "concubinage." Finally, unmarried sex, for the purpose of this book, will be defined as two single people having consensual sex.

Important Things to Know

Before venturing further, we should note that the Hebrew word *iysh* can mean man, men, husband, husbands, male, males, human, or father. Likewise, the Hebrew word *ishshah* can mean woman, women, mother, mothers, wife, wives, and female. This is also true for the Greek word for "man" and "woman," so it is of the utmost importance that we take the context into consideration before determining which word should be properly used at any given time.

Another word we will come across is the Hebrew word *karath*, which is mostly translated as "cut off"; other versions have used "excommunicated," which has caused quite some confusion. However, when comparing scripture with scripture, we can determine it means "death." *Strong's Concordance* defines *karath* as "cutoff, cut down, asunder, destroy, or consume." Compromising Christians, who are always looking to make the scriptures acceptable, have chosen to use the more palatable "excommunicated" instead. The obvious problem is that there isn't one example in scripture of people being expelled outside of Israel. Christians who hold to the excommunicated view cannot show one instance of an incestuous couple being expelled outside of Israel. Why? When God gave Israel his law and told them that the heathen nations were being punished (Lev. 18: 24–30) for breaking these laws, why would he let an incestuous couple continue to commit sin outside of Israel, when judgment always begins in the house of the Lord (1 Pet. 4:17)? However, there is plenty of evidence to the contrary.

> And the Lord spake unto Moses, saying, Speak thou also unto the children of Israel, saying, Verily my sabbaths ye shall keep: for it is a sign between me and you throughout your generations; that ye may know that I am the Lord that doth sanctify you. Ye shall keep the sabbath therefore; for it is holy unto you: every one that defileth it shall surely be put to death: for whosoever doeth any work therein, that soul shall be cut off from among his people. (Exod. 31:12–14)

> And while the children of Israel were in the wilderness, they found a man that gathered sticks upon the sabbath day. And they that found him gathering sticks brought him unto Moses and Aaron, and unto all the congregation. And they put him in ward, because it was not declared what should be done to him. And the Lord said unto Moses, The man shall be surely put to death: all the congregation shall stone him with stones without the camp. And all the congregation brought him without the camp, and stoned him with stones, and he died; as the Lord commanded Moses. (Num. 15:32–36)

This should be enough to convince any reasonable-minded person that *karath* meant "death"; however, we will look at a few more instances of the over 280 times when *karath* is used to further prove our point. Genesis 9:11 says, "And I will establish my covenant with you; neither shall all flesh be cut off any more by the waters of a flood; neither shall there any more be a flood to destroy [*karath*] the earth." Did God mean that mankind was excommunicated? Scripture tells us that only eight souls were saved (1 Pet. 3:20), so it should be clear that *karath* means "perish or destroyed." Here are more examples:

- *Karath* is translated as "made" and is used in conjunction with *beriyth*, the Hebrew word for "covenant" (Gen. 15:18; 21:32).
- A male was *karath* for not having his foreskin circumcised (Gen. 17:14).
- Joseph told Pharaoh to store the surplus of the land so the land wouldn't be *karath* through the famine (Gen. 41:36).
- People who ate leavened bread during the Feast of Unleavened Bread were *karath* (Exod. 12:15, 19).
- God told the Israelites to break the pagans' images and *karath* their groves (Exod. 34:13).
- Anyone who touched a dead body and didn't cleanse himself or herself was *karath* (Num. 19:13).

CHAPTER 1

Covetousness/Lust/Desire, Masturbation, and Nudity

EXODUS 20:17 SAYS, "THOU SHALT not covet." This verse is clear, concise, and straightforward, so why does it generate so much confusion? Perhaps it's because so many fail to grasp Jesus's words in relation to God's law, causing them to mistakenly believe the law in relation to coveting has been expanded. Bogged down in semantics, too many people believe lust means only something that is sinful; however, we'll see that the Hebrew and Greek word for "covet" or "lust" is, in fact, neutral. We must take the context into account to determine whether sin has occurred.

Keep in mind that most Bible versions aren't consistent when translating the Hebrew and Greek words *chamad* and *epithumeo*, respectively. This is why when you study the scriptures, I recommend that you use a literal translation such as Young's or Rotherham's Bible. Robert Young consistently translates *chamad* and *epithumeo* as "desire," which erases many doctrinal misconceptions and confusion so many other Bible translations create when they use several different words for one Hebrew and Greek word, such as "lust," "desire," or "covet." The following is from *Young's Literal Translation of the Bible* (YLT):

Ex 20:14 Thou dost not commit adultery.

Ex 20:17 Thou dost not desire the house of thy neighbor, thou not desire the wife of thy neighbor, or his man-servant, or his handmaid or his ox, or his ass, or anything which is thy neighbor's.

Matt 5:28 but I—I say to you, that every one who is looking on a woman to desire her, did already commit adultery with her in his heart.

From reading these verses it is clear that the word "desire" is used in a negative context for sin. Again, Jesus didn't create a new rule to be obeyed but was simply affirming the law against unlawful desiring or—to put it in a more familiar way—coveting. Further analysis reveals that the Exodus 20:17 coveting law Jesus mentioned was used against adultery, found in verse 14.

Don't commit adultery (Exod. 20:14). = Don't have sex with another man's wife.

Don't desire your neighbor's wife (Exod. 20:17). = Don't desire to have sex with your neighbor's wife.

Don't steal (Exod. 20:15). = Don't take something that belongs to someone else.

Don't desire anything that is your neighbor's (Exod. 20:17). = Don't desire to steal anything that is your neighbor's.

Let's consider an example. Bob's neighbor, John, has a brand-new red Chevrolet Corvette Z71 convertible. Bob likes John's car. One day while Bob reclines in his lawn chair, he fantasizes about driving John's car. Did Bob sin? No, he didn't sin. Now, let's say that Bob sees John's car parked outside, and he knows John isn't home. Bob decides to steal John's car, so

Covetousness/Lust/Desire, Masturbation, and Nudity

he walks outside toward John's car, but before he can pick the lock, he sees John driving in his other car, heading home. Bob just plays it off by walking right past John's car. John has no idea his car was about to be broken into and stolen; he thinks Bob was just taking an afternoon walk.

Did Bob sin? Yes. The reason Bob sinned is that he desired to steal John's car; it doesn't matter that he didn't actually steal his car. What's important is Bob's intent to steal—hence the commandment against desiring (coveting). Even though there was no sacrifice for the sin of holding a forbidden desire, it was still a sin because the individual intended to commit the act, which in this case was stealing, which in fact did require the shedding of blood. With God's law, opportunity isn't needed to sin, only the intent to do so. So we can safely say that Bob's unsuccessful attempt doesn't mean he's in the clear with God on this issue.

Now, armed with this information, let's change the scenario. Bob notices John's wife, Lucy, at the beach; she wears a string bikini. Bob thinks she's beautiful. Did Bob sin? No. What if Bob got an erection? Nope. What if Bob thought about having sex with Lucy while he masturbated? No, he still hasn't sinned; just because he fantasized about having sex with John's wife doesn't mean he would actually have had sex with her. Now, what if John is out of town on a business trip and Bob makes sexual advances toward Lucy? In such a scenario, Bob did sin regardless of the response from Lucy. This is because he desired to have sex with another man's wife, which God's law forbids.

As for the act of masturbation itself, it was never condemned in the Old Testament; one would simply be unclean for the day. Deuteronomy 23:9–11 speaks of being unclean through emission; no detail is given, so one must conclude that this broad term included nocturnal emission, masturbation, and sex. Recall that uncleanness wasn't in and of itself sinful; the sin was disobeying God's command to cleanse oneself. The most common proof text is to say that *porneia* includes masturbation, despite the lack of evidence to make such a claim. There are still a few people out there who desperately cling to the sin of Onan as a condemnation of masturbation. However, Onan's downfall was radically different from masturbation.

Judah told his son Onan to marry Tamar, his sister-in-law, after his brother Er died (Gen. 38:8). This would later be known as the Levite marriage vow Israel practiced. Apparently Onan had absolutely no problem with having sex with Tamar, but when it came to having to impregnate her, he made sure to ejaculate after he pulled out of her (Gen. 38:9). Onan's sin was his selfishness in not wanting to share any inheritance Judah left, because Tamar's children would have been considered his dead brother's and not his. He also lied because the whole point of agreeing to marry Tamar was to give her children so she could be supported when she got older. Onan committed *coitus interruptus*, not masturbation; God killed him because of his selfishness and lying.

By comparing scripture with scripture, we can see that people who use the word *porneia*, found in the New Testament, as a proof text for masturbation run into a major problem. Why was this practice allowed in the Old Testament but not in the New? "Ye shall not add unto the word which I command you, neither shall ye diminish ought from it, that ye may keep the commandments of the Lord your God which I command you" (Deut. 4:2).

One cannot make a sound biblical claim that masturbation was once allowed but is now condemned. Neither do critics have any evidence in the Old Testament to show that masturbation is a sin, which leads to the Deuteronomy 4:2 conundrum. Most Christians don't have a problem saying that someone has something nice or beautiful; that wouldn't be sinful. No one would think someone was committing sin just by telling another person that he or she has a nice car or fantasizing about driving it. Most would say, however, that it would be a sin if someone stole, damaged, or even tried to steal or damage another person's car.

Yet, they think a man who becomes sexually aroused at the sight of a beautiful woman who isn't his wife (even if she is his wife, some may argue) is sinning and that a woman who becomes sexually aroused by a man other than her husband is sinning. It just goes to show that there's a plethora of Christians who don't even understand what adultery is. As we'll see in a later chapter, a man cannot commit adultery with a single woman, and a single woman cannot commit adultery, regardless of the man's marital status. Still, some Christians persist that a single man's desiring (or, as they would say, lusting) after a single woman is adultery. Ignorance of God's law is never a good thing and always leads to more problems.

Some believers say masturbation isn't a sin but that fantasizing about a nude person is. It's surprising and tragic that so many Christians think nudity is a sin despite the fact that we're all born naked. Genesis 1:31 says, "God saw everything he had made and said it was very good." This would include Adam and Eve. Genesis 2:25 says, "They were naked but not ashamed," yet how could this be possible if they were naked? We will see that when scripture speaks of nudity, it presents it in a negative way only in terms of shame. Adam and Eve sewed fig leaves to cover their nakedness as a result of eating the forbidden fruit, not because they were naked. If nakedness itself was the problem, why didn't they cover themselves *prior* to eating the forbidden fruit? Why didn't God give Adam and Eve clothes and then declare that everything he'd made was very good?

The issue here is that nudity isn't a sin; if someone had walked around naked in ancient Israel, nothing would have happened to him or her; no shedding of blood was required. Critics might mention the fact that Adam and Eve clothed themselves when they knew they were naked and that God killed an animal and made them animal skins to wear. It's true that an animal's blood was shed to cover their sin, but their sin was eating the forbidden fruit, not being naked. Besides, to proclaim that Adam and Eve's nakedness was sin is to say that God created them in sin. Genesis 3:7 says, "And the eyes of them both were opened, and they knew that they were naked; and they sewed fig leaves together, and made themselves aprons." Their sin led to shame, and they hid themselves from God.

But did Adam and Eve actually make aprons out of fig leaves? No, the Hebrew word for "apron" is *chgowr*, which actually means "girdle or belt"; this is the proper translation used in *Young's Literal Translation*. The KJV translators didn't want to inform their readers that Eve was still bare breasted, even after realizing she was naked. This was just too much for them to "bare" (pun intended). So instead of "belt," the KJV translators stated that *chgowr* is an "apron"; in fact, this was the only time they translated the word as such.

For far too many years, Christians in the Western world have allowed their cultural taboos to equate with God's holy Word. That is, their standards are better than God's. No one would ever make such an explicit statement, but we can implicitly know their beliefs by reading their materials in regard to nudity. Many cultures even today don't have a problem with women being bare breasted in public; to them it's no different from a man going topless. Christians should respect other people's culture, provided it doesn't break any of God's law; this would include women being topless. Christian missionaries led the charge against the "sinful" Hawaiian hula dance because it was originally done topless, yet there isn't one scripture that forbids such an activity. The important lesson here is not to let your own cultural preferences be used to condemn practices you don't like.

Some Westerners tend to be hypocrites at heart. While looking down on Third World countries, where women still roam bare breasted in public, they pass laws that outlaw breastfeeding in public. At the same time, they allow see-through tops or shirts so tight you can see the nipple impression. The scriptures portray nakedness in a negative light only in terms of unpreparedness that leads to shame. Revelation 16:15 says, "Behold, I come as a thief. Blessed is he that watcheth, and keepeth his garments, lest he walk naked, and they see his shame."

Jesus said to be on guard for his return and to be prepared; he compared people who aren't prepared with people walking around naked due to their unpreparedness. This example is similar to a father telling his son to clean his room while he runs some errands and promises to take him to the mall if his room is clean; but when the father returns, he finds his son still watching TV, and his room is still dirty. The sin is the fact that the son didn't clean his room; he disobeyed his father and was unprepared. Watching TV was just a vehicle used in disobeying a command. Revelation 16:15 uses being naked as proof of being unprepared and thus being ashamed as a result of nakedness.

Covetousness/Lust/Desire, Masturbation, and Nudity

In Genesis 9:22, Ham saw his father, Noah, who was drunk and naked; he then told his brothers, Shem and Japheth, who walked backward and covered their father's nakedness. When Noah realized what had happened, he cursed Ham's son Canaan; it is clear from these scriptures that Noah was drunk and naked, facts that brought him shame. Ham had no intention of covering his father's shame, but instead he told his two brothers about their father's drunken nakedness as ridicule. That some people spin this story as a condemnation of nudity is ludicrous; Noah's sin was drunkenness. The fact that he was naked and drunk compounded his sin, but if he'd been nude and not drunk, do you think that Ham would've told his brothers?

Too many people use their Western culture as a proof text for scripture. Indeed, it was very common at the time for people to be seen nude; private bathing is a rather recent phenomenon. This would have been true in Moses's time and even during Jesus's ministry; when the law mentioned seeing the "nakedness" of a relative, it was denoted in a sexual way (Lev. 18:6–17) because seeing someone naked wasn't uncommon. One shouldn't be surprised considering most inhabitants of this planet live off two dollars a day or less; they don't have the luxury of taking a private bath. It's complete nonsense to assume that the ancient Hebrews (and many people today) could even afford such a luxury, when they most likely couldn't.

Exodus 32:25 says,

And when Moses saw that the people were naked; (for
Aaron had made them naked unto their shame among their
enemies:) Then Moses stood in the gate of the camp, and
said, Who is on the LORD's side? let him come to me. And
all the sons of Levi gathered themselves together to him.

The "nakedness" mentioned here was more than just nudity; it more than likely included sexual idolatry, since some people used sex as a form of worship to the golden calf.

Second Samuel 6:14–23 says,

And David danced before the Lord with all his might; and David was girded with a linen ephod. So David and all the house of Israel brought up the ark of the Lord with shouting, and with the sound of the trumpet. And as the ark of the Lord came into the city of David, Michal Saul's daughter looked through a window, and saw king David leaping and dancing before the Lord; and she despised him in her heart. And they brought in the ark of the Lord, and set it in his place, in the midst of the tabernacle that David had pitched for it: and David offered burnt offerings and peace offerings before the Lord. And as soon as David had made an end of offering burnt offerings and peace offerings, he blessed the people in the name of the Lord of hosts. And he dealt among all the people, even among the whole multitude of Israel, as well to the women as men, to every one a cake of bread, and a good piece of flesh, and a flagon of wine. So all the people departed every one to his house. Then David returned to bless his household. And Michal the daughter of Saul came out to meet David, and said, How glorious was the king of Israel to day, who uncovered himself to day in the eyes of the handmaids of his servants, as one of the vain fellows shamelessly uncovereth himself! And David said unto Michal, It was before the Lord, which chose me before thy father, and before all his house, to appoint me ruler over the people of the Lord, over Israel: therefore will I play before the Lord. And I will yet be more vile than thus, and will be base in mine own sight: and of the maidservants which thou hast spoken of, of them shall I be had in honour. Therefore Michal the daughter of Saul had no child unto the day of her death.

During the reign of David, most people didn't wear underwear beneath their garments, and King David was no exception. An ephod was a sleeveless garment extended just beyond the hips or waist; this is what he wore. When he danced out of excitement for the return of the ark of the Lord, he exposed his genitals to the people. This, in turn, caused Michal, David's wife, who saw this incident transpire from the window of her living quarters, to despise David for doing such a thing before his servants. The only one wrong in this episode was Michal, who despised David for exposing himself in front of other women. God had no problem with David's exposing himself during his dance—a crucial point. Note that the scriptures mention absolutely nothing about God's cursing Michal to be childless. Only David rebuked her (2 Sam. 6:21–22), and verse 23 says she had no children until the day of her death.

Another incident involving nakedness and David is in 2 Samuel 11:2: "And it came to pass in an eveningtide, that David arose from off his bed, and walked upon the roof of the king's house: and from the roof he saw a woman washing herself; and the woman was very beautiful to look upon."

David didn't sin by simply looking at Bathsheba as she bathed herself; voyeurism isn't a sin. Neither did Bathsheba sin by bathing in public. The sin that resulted in God's cursing David was adultery and murder. While it's true that the sin of adultery always starts by looking, which David was guilty of doing, it cannot be said that every man who looks at a married woman will commit adultery with her; such an inference would be incorrect.

Isaiah 20:2–4 says,

> At the same time spake the Lord by Isaiah the son of Amoz, saying, Go and loose the sackcloth from off thy loins, and put off thy shoe from thy foot. And he did so, walking naked and barefoot. And the Lord said, Like as my servant Isaiah hath walked naked and barefoot three years for a sign and wonder upon Egypt and upon Ethiopia; So shall the king of Assyria lead away the Egyptians prisoners, and the Ethiopians captives, young and old, naked and barefoot, even with their buttocks uncovered, to the shame of Egypt.

No Christian would argue that God can sin; the very idea is utterly ludicrous. So we can safely say that God's telling Isaiah to go naked for three years wasn't a sin. Once again, nudity is connected with shame—the shame the Egyptians and Ethiopians felt when the Assyrians took them captive. Prisoners or captives of all wars in mankind's history experienced shame, whether or not they were clothed. Who would feel proud if they were defeated and led away into captivity? God told Isaiah to prophesy naked as a sign that the Egyptians and Ethiopians would be taken captive naked.

The Spirit of the Lord fell on Saul, and he prophesied; he even prophesied in front of Samuel naked, which led to people wondering whether Saul was among the prophets (1 Sam. 19:23–24). Seemingly it was common for God's prophets to prophesy in the nude. Regarding the Hebrew language, in this instance *Rotherham's Emphasized Bible* (REB) translates the Hebrew word for "clothes," *beged*, as "upper garments." The Hebrew word for "naked," *arown*, is translated as "prostrate," which insinuates that Saul was only shirtless and lying prostrate before Samuel. In reality he was lying naked before Samuel. To summarize nudity it is best to quote Paul who said, "In like manner also, that women adorn themselves in modest apparel, with modesty and sobriety; not with braided hair, or gold, or pearls, or costly array" (1 Tim. 2:9). As Christians we are called to dress modestly. This means one would dress differently depending on the occasion: work, beach, party, or fellowshipping with other Christians. However, this in no way condemns nudity as sin. Showing up to work in your pajamas would be inappropriate but not sin.

Pornography

This discussion brings us to the issue of pornography. The reality is that pornography—like alcohol, television, food, the Internet, and other things—can become a sin if one is addicted to it. Christians must always practice moderation (Phil. 4:5), as self-control is one of the fruits of the Spirit (Gal. 5:22–23). As we've already seen, masturbation isn't a sin, and desire (lust) depends on the intent. We've also seen that nudity isn't a sin either; neither is voyeurism. That's right; there isn't one instance in scripture that condemns voyeurism. If Bob wanted to release his sexual hormones by watching a pornographic video or photo, he wouldn't be sinning. Being a voyeur or watching people have sex or be nude isn't a sin any more than watching a robbery or documentary on war. Besides, there was very little privacy in biblical times, so seeing a couple have sex wouldn't have come as a shock. When King Abimelech saw Isaac sporting Rebekah, he was shocked because he thought they were brother and sister (Gen. 26:8); more than likely it wasn't the first time he saw a couple have sex. Ironically, Christians don't have a problem watching sins on TV or the Internet, such as beatings, killings, thefts, drunkenness, and so forth. However, for some reason, pornography is sudden cause for alarm. There are some Christians who hold the view that nude art is fine but that pornography is sin. But this view is entirely arbitrary. Who gets to decide what is art and what is pornography?

The Greek word *porneia* literally means the things prostitutes do. However, in scripture it refers to illicit sex, and the Bible doesn't know of anything (there is no clear definition of it) we define today as pornography. "I know it when I see it." That famous quote from a former US Supreme Court Justice, Potter Stewart, was an attempt to define hardcore pornography in 1964. Eventually the Supreme Court grew tired of looking at various films and determining whether they were obscene. Pornography is nothing more than a man-made construct that is hard to define. Some people believe nudity is porn, so does this mean doctors are into porn? Others, Christians included, have no problem with nude art, whether it's a painting or sculpture. But what about nude models and nude photography? How is this any different? Is it OK for a woman to pose nude for a sculpture or painting but not for a picture? If not, why not? If you don't have a problem with that, what would be wrong if she were photographed playing with a dildo?

Instead of focusing on a man-made construct like pornography, Christians should focus on what is sinful and what isn't, as God's Word clearly defines it. We should be silent, even as God is, on the topic of so-called pornography and speak out against actual sexual sins. Some of the oldest forms of pornography, where graphically detailed descriptions were made, were described in books written in the Victorian era. Most people mistakenly believe pornography is confined to paintings, pictures, or video but not to books. If pornography is sin, then it shouldn't be in the scriptures; on the other hand, if it isn't sin, then there is no conflict whatsoever if graphic language is being used.

There can be no denying the fact that God employed such graphic language in the holy scriptures. For example, God rebuked his wife Israel and told of her sins in Ezekiel 16:16–34.

> And of thy garments thou didst take, and deckedst thy high places with divers colours, and playedst the harlot thereupon: the like things shall not come, neither shall it be so. [17] Thou hast also taken thy fair jewels of my gold and of my silver, which I had given thee, and madest to thyself images of men, and didst commit whoredom with them, [18] And tookest thy broidered garments, and coveredst them: and thou hast set mine oil and mine incense before them. [19] My meat also which I gave thee, fine flour, and oil, and honey, wherewith I fed thee, thou hast even set it before them for a sweet savour: and thus it was, saith the Lord God. [20] Moreover thou hast taken thy sons and thy daughters, whom thou hast borne unto me, and these hast thou sacrificed unto them to be devoured. Is this of thy whoredoms a small matter, [21] That thou hast slain my children, and delivered them to cause them to pass through the fire for them? [22] And in all thine abominations and thy whoredoms thou hast not remembered the days of thy youth, when thou wast naked and bare, and wast polluted in thy blood. [23] And it came to pass after all thy wickedness, (woe, woe unto thee! saith the Lord God;) [24] That thou hast also built unto thee an eminent place, and hast made thee an high place in every street. [25] Thou hast built thy high place at every head of the way, and hast made thy beauty to be abhorred, and hast opened thy feet to every one that passed by, and multiplied thy whoredoms. [26] Thou hast also committed fornication with the Egyptians thy neighbours, great of flesh; and hast increased thy whoredoms, to provoke me to anger. [27] Behold, therefore I have stretched out my hand over thee, and have diminished thine ordinary food, and

delivered thee unto the will of them that hate thee, the daughters of the Philistines, which are ashamed of thy lewd way. [28] Thou hast played the whore also with the Assyrians, because thou wast unsatiable; yea, thou hast played the harlot with them, and yet couldest not be satisfied. [29] Thou hast moreover multiplied thy fornication in the land of Canaan unto Chaldea; and yet thou wast not satisfied herewith. [30] How weak is thine heart, saith the Lord God, seeing thou doest all these things, the work of an imperious whorish woman; [31] In that thou buildest thine eminent place in the head of every way, and makest thine high place in every street; and hast not been as an harlot, in that thou scornest hire; [32] But as a wife that committeth adultery, which taketh strangers instead of her husband! [33] They give gifts to all whores: but thou givest thy gifts to all thy lovers, and hirest them, that they may come unto thee on every side for thy whoredom. [34] And the contrary is in thee from other women in thy whoredoms, whereas none followeth thee to commit whoredoms: and in that thou givest a reward, and no reward is given unto thee, therefore thou art contrary.

For those who might not understand some of the language used here, the images (v. 17) Israel made were none other than dildos. God stated that his wife Israel had committed whoredom with the Egyptians, her neighbor of great flesh. Of course, "flesh" here refers to the penis. God stated that even the Philistines were ashamed of her lewd ways (v. 27). She also played the whore with the Assyrians and Canaanites; despite this, she wasn't satisfied. God called her an "imperious whorish woman" (v. 30); he said she wasn't a prostitute because they had sex for money, but she was like an adulteress; instead of receiving gifts from her lovers, she gave gifts to them (vv. 31–34). That they might come unto her on every side for her whoredom (v. 33), God said she went out of her way to pay with gifts the men she had sex with, even though she got none in return (v. 34).

The passage says that she spread her feet at everyone who passed by and multiplied her whoredom (v. 25). Of course, someone cannot spread his or her feet; the Hebrew word for "feet" is sometimes used as a euphemism for genitalia. In this case it refers to the vagina. So what God said here is that she opened her vagina and had sex with every man who approached her. In an attempt to water down the scriptures and be less graphic, some translations use "legs" instead of "feet"; either way the Hebrew word denotes genitalia.

Ezekiel 23:1–22 says,

> The word of the Lord came again unto me, saying, Son of man, there were two women, the daughters of one mother: And they committed whoredoms in Egypt; they committed whoredoms in their youth: there were their breasts pressed, and there they bruised the teats of their virginity. And the names of them were Aholah the elder, and Aholibah her sister: and they were mine, and they bare sons and daughters. Thus were their names; Samaria is Aholah, and Jerusalem Aholibah. And Aholah played the harlot when she was mine; and she doted on her lovers, on the Assyrians her neighbours, Which were clothed with blue, captains and rulers, all of them desirable young men, horsemen riding upon horses. Thus she committed her whoredoms with them, with all them that were the chosen men of Assyria, and with all on whom she doted: with all their idols she defiled herself. Neither left she her whoredoms brought from Egypt: for in her youth they lay with her, and they bruised the breasts of her virginity, and poured their whoredom upon her. Wherefore I have delivered her into the hand of her lovers, into the hand of the Assyrians, upon whom she doted. These discovered her nakedness: they took her sons and her daughters, and slew her with the sword: and she became famous among women; for they had executed judgment upon her. And when her sister Aholibah saw this, she was more corrupt in her inordinate love than she, and in her whoredoms more than her sister in her whoredoms. She doted upon the Assyrians her neighbours, captains and rulers clothed most gorgeously, horsemen riding upon horses, all of them desirable young men. Then

Covetousness/Lust/Desire, Masturbation, and Nudity

I saw that she was defiled, that they took both one way, And that she increased her whoredoms: for when she saw men pourtrayed upon the wall, the images of the Chaldeans pourtrayed with vermilion, Girded with girdles upon their loins, exceeding in dyed attire upon their heads, all of them princes to look to, after the manner of the Babylonians of Chaldea, the land of their nativity: And as soon as she saw them with her eyes, she doted upon them, and sent messengers unto them into Chaldea. And the Babylonians came to her into the bed of love, and they defiled her with their whoredom, and she was polluted with them, and her mind was alienated from them. So she discovered her whoredoms, and discovered her nakedness: then my mind was alienated from her, like as my mind was alienated from her sister. Yet she multiplied her whoredoms, in calling to remembrance the days of her youth, wherein she had played the harlot in the land of Egypt. For she doted upon their paramours, whose flesh is as the flesh of asses, and whose issue is like the issue of horses. Thus thou calledst to remembrance the lewdness of thy youth, in bruising thy teats by the Egyptians for the paps of thy youth.

The word "doted" (*agab*) is defined as "sensual love or a very strong desire," according to *Strong's Concordance*. Both Aholah and Aholibah were guilty of this desire, since they were both married to God. Aholah's sister, Aholibah, was even more corrupt than her sister and was so sex obsessed that when she saw images of Chaldean men on the wall, she had to commit adultery with them (v. 14). The word "flesh" or "members" is just another euphemism for penis, and "issue" refers to semen (v. 20).

In Galatians 5:12, Paul became upset about people obeying the law of circumcision, so upset in fact that he recommended cutting off the entire penis instead of just cutting off the foreskin. It is indeed true that Christians have gotten puritanical over the years in regard to sex, so much so that the translators purposefully don't use the best English words available when it comes to the original Hebrew words for genitalia, even when those words appear in a letter from an apostle.

The Song of Songs is a book about sexual romance and eroticism between unmarried lovers that can also be considered pornographic. The reason we know they were unmarried is that they made love in her mother's house in the bed where she was conceived (Song 3:4). They refer to each other as lovers and aren't husband and wife until much later. Song of Songs 5:16 says, "His mouth is most sweet: yea, he is altogether lovely." The word translated as "mouth," *chek*, means "tasting," "palate," or "inside of the mouth." Song of Songs 1:2 uses the word *peh* for "mouth," so we can deduce that French kissing is mentioned throughout the Song of Songs (Song 5:16; 7:9).

Song of Songs 7:1–5 says,

> How beautiful are thy feet in sandals O daughter of a noble. The curvings of thy hips are like ornaments wrought by the hands of a skilled workman. Thy navel is a round bowl, may it not lack spiced wine! Thy body a heap of wheat fenced about with lilies; Thy two breasts are like two young roes the twins of a gazelle: Thy neck is like a tower of ivory, Thine eyes are pools in Heshbon by the gate of Bath-rabbim, Thy nose is like the tower of Lebanon which looketh towards Damascus: Thy head upon thee is like Carmel, And the hair of thy head is like purple, The king is held captive by the ringlets! (REB)

The Hebrew word for "navel," *shorer*, can also mean "vulva." It's absurd to state that a navel can produce a liquid substance; however, if "navel" actually means "vulva," then the "wine" makes sense. By comparing scripture with scripture, we see that in the first verse he described her feet, legs, and thighs; he then described her vulva and said "may it not lack spiced wine" (v. 7). The "wine" he referred to is simply ejaculation fluid; in this same verse, he said her belly is like a heap of wheat set about the lilies. The Hebrew word for "belly," *beten*, would make translating *shorer* as "navel" redundant, so it must refer to her vulva instead. The fact that he clearly described her from bottom to top, describing her breasts in verse 3 and ending with her head in verse 5, further proves the point that "navel" in this instance is a euphemism for "vulva." Some of the newer Bible translations, which claim to be true to the original autographs, still fail to tell it like it actually is in the Hebrew.

Moving on, Song of Songs 2:3 says, "As the apple tree among the trees of the wood, so is my beloved among the sons. I sat down under his shadow with great delight, and his fruit was sweet to my taste." Some Christians say Song of Songs 2:3 cryptically refers to oral sex, but there's nothing cryptic about it—it quite plainly refers to oral sex. In fact, critics have no rational way of explaining this verse. She sat under his shadow with great delight, and his fruit was sweet to her taste or palate, because the Hebrew word *chek* (taste) is being used again.

Song of Songs 8:1–2 says,

> O that thou wert as my brother, that sucked the breasts of my mother! [when] I should find thee without, I would kiss thee; yea, I should not be despised. I would lead thee, and bring thee into my mother's house, who would instruct me: I would cause thee to drink of spiced wine of the juice of my pomegranate.

By comparing scripture with scripture, we know he said, "May her vulva not lack spiced wine" (Song 7:2), so it should be clear that she referred to her vulva as a pomegranate fruit, and to drink from it is referred to oral sex, vaginal sex, or both.

This book isn't intended to be a treatise of the Song of Songs; the goal is to show the reader just how ridiculous, arbitrary, and continually evolving is the definition of pornography. Christians who want to stick with the predominant view of pornography must admit that the Bible itself is pornographic; further, saying that the Song of Songs is symbolic for Christ's love for believers doesn't address their problem and is simply an evasion. One would think God could have demonstrated his feelings for Israel in a less graphic manner, yet he did not do so.

Before ending this chapter, let us go over one more verse from the Song of Songs. "We have a little sister, and she hath no breasts: what shall we do for our sister in the day when she shall be spoken for?" (8:8). Can anyone please tell us what this verse symbolizes in relation to Christ's love for believers? The author would love to know what the spiritual meaning is for those who insist that the Song of Songs is more than just a book on sex. What is the significance of her little sister having no breasts?

CHAPTER 2

Adultery, Polygyny, and Divorce

IN EXODUS 20:14, DEUTERONOMY 5:18, and Leviticus 18:20, God defines adultery as a man having sex with another man's wife, or a man who divorces his wife and marries another woman (Mal. 2:16; Luke 16:18). Adultery of the heart is when a man desires to have another man's wife regardless of his success in carrying out his sinful desire, as we discussed in the previous chapter. As we'll see, it's impossible for a single woman to commit adultery—at no time is a single woman ever condemned for adultery in scripture; neither is it possible for a single man to commit adultery with a single woman. Let's not confuse man's laws with God's, because we will be judged by his laws, not by man's.

Adultery required the shedding of blood and is mentioned with several sexual sins that were an abomination and caused the land to be defiled (Lev. 18:27). One of the most common excuses against adultery is that God needed to preserve a line for the Messiah. There are two problems with this view. First, if God had just wanted to preserve the line of the Messiah, he could have easily applied the laws forbidding adultery only against Judah, since he wouldn't come from the other eleven lines. Second, it would have made no difference had God done this. Had God fertilized Mary's egg, Jesus would have been conceived in sin like everyone else. When the scriptures mention a "seed" in Mary, it refers not only to sperm but also to the ovary. Besides, anyone who studies the scriptures knows that even with God's law, Israel still chose to break them, thus polluting their genealogy and defiling the land.

People who try to justify adultery and/or swapping partners purposefully conflate adultery with stealing; when permission is given from a spouse, they argue, then adultery isn't taking place. After all, borrowing something from someone isn't stealing. The problem is that when a man has sex with another man's wife, he's mixing his seed. Adultery is marital adulteration regardless of whether a spouse gives permission. God created marriage and set the rules on whether one violates the marriage covenant. At no time is adultery ever permitted under any circumstance. God isn't the author of confusion (1 Cor. 14:33), so how could God be married to Israel, call her an adulteress, and yet approve of couples swapping their spouses?

It wasn't OK to swap spouses or to sleep with another man's wife; that's why Joseph ran from Potiphar's wife rather than committing adultery (Gen. 39:7–12). Abraham told Pharaoh that Sarah was his sister, leaving out the fact that she was also his wife; God inflicted leprosy on Pharaoh to prevent adultery (Gen. 12:11–20). The same event happened again (Gen. 20:1–18). God told Abimelech in a dream that Sarah was married and that he would die if he went "near" her. Abimelech, much like Pharaoh, knew adultery was wrong and didn't want to commit the act; neither one even tried to ask for Abraham's permission when they found out he was married to Sarah. When the situation was eventually resolved, God opened the wombs of his wife and harem, so even heathen rulers knew adultery was wrong.

Much like Israel's committing spiritual adultery by worshipping other gods (idolatry), or someone claiming to be a Christian married to Christ but serving another (1 Cor. 6:15), there's no way to get around marital adulteration. An impotent husband cannot have his friend have sex with his wife so they can have a child. There is no case law for a reverse Levite vow, and the laws defining adultery strictly prohibit polyandry (one wife with multiple husbands).

Some believe that women and men are equal in the New Testament; however, the scriptures teach that the woman was created for the man, not the man for the woman (1 Cor. 11:9). Galatians 3:28 is often used as a proof text of equality between the sexes, but when it is read in context, one comes away with a different view.

> For ye are all the children of God by faith in Christ Jesus. For as many of you as have been baptized into Christ have put on Christ. There is neither Jew nor Greek, there is neither bond nor free, there is neither male nor female: for ye are all one in Christ Jesus. And if ye be Christ's, then are ye Abraham's seed, and heirs according to the promise. (Gal. 3:26–29)

Paul talked about how our salvation is in Christ and our relationship with God is equal as a result of Christ's death and resurrection. People who use this as a proof text usually ignore verses 26–27. They go straight to verse 28, thus ignoring Paul's context. First Corinthians 11:3, 8–9 says,

> But I would have you know, that the head of every man is Christ; and the head of the woman is the man; and the head of Christ is God… For the man is not of the woman: but the woman of the man. Neither was the man created for the woman; but the woman for the man.

Ephesians 5:22–24 says,

> Wives, submit yourselves unto your own husbands, as unto the Lord. For the husband is the head of the wife, even as Christ is the head of the church: and he is the saviour of the body. Therefore as the church is subject unto Christ, so let the wives be to their own husbands in every thing.

It's important to understand the doctrine of headship before delving into polygyny, since we've already seen that Jesus didn't add to or take away from God's law. Doing so would have created a whole host of problems and contradictions. An occasional argument against polygyny is Mark 10:12, which states that if a wife divorces her husband and marries another, she commits adultery. However, just because a wife could divorce her husband (there was no possibility for a wife to divorce her husband under the Mosaic exception) doesn't mean Jesus nullified God's creation order. It just means men and women could both be guilty of committing adultery. Likewise, a child who sins by lying isn't equal with his or her parents in authority just because he or she can be guilty of lying; this proves only that children and their parents can sin by lying.

The typical types of Christians who are against polygyny are as follows:

1. Christians who don't read the Bible.
2. Christians who read the Bible but do so in light of what the traditions of men have taught them.
3. Christians who think polygyny is primitive and find its presence in the Bible embarrassing. They want to show the secular world that Christianity is culturally relevant.

One of the most common scriptures cited against polygyny is Matthew 19:4–5.

> And he answered and said unto them, Have ye not read, that he which made them at the beginning made them male and female, And said, For this cause shall a man leave father and mother, and shall cleave to his wife: and they twain shall be one flesh?

This is what the author refers to as the "peephole method"; the peephole method is analogous to someone walking around and holding a square cardboard cutout in front of his or her face; all he or she can see is through the peephole. It goes without saying that anyone who tries to see through a peephole is going to have major problems walking around and is bound to stumble. Looking through a peephole can be no different when studying scripture. One example unbelievers refer to most is Matthew 10:34. "Think not that I am come to send peace on earth: I came not to send peace, but a sword."

The peephole method in this case is designed to make Jesus look like a violent revolutionary. But is this actually the case?

> For the word of God is quick, and powerful, and sharper than any twoedged sword, piercing even to the dividing asunder of soul and spirit, and of the joints and marrow, and is a discerner of the thoughts and intents of the heart. (Heb. 4:12)

> [T]he sword of the Spirit, which is the word of God. (Eph. 6:17)

> Repent; or else I will come unto thee quickly, and will fight against them with the sword of my mouth. (Rev. 2:16)

When the peephole is removed, one can determine that the scriptures speak of the Word of God as a sword. It's rather unfortunate that it's not just unbelievers but also believers who employ the peephole method, and many who do so purposefully ignore scriptures that would refute their doctrine.

Now let's return to Matthew 19:4–5. Instead of looking through the peephole, let's throw it in the trash. Rather than looking at just a few isolated verses through the peephole, we can now use our full vision to see the totality of what scripture says. Matthew 19:3 says, "The Pharisees also came unto him, tempting him, and saying unto him, Is it lawful for a man to put away his wife for every cause?"

We can now see that Jesus wasn't talking about polygyny; the Pharisees asked Jesus about divorce, and he spent verses 4–12 giving his answer to the Pharisees and later the disciples. The fact that critics of polygyny often use this as their greatest proof text is evidence enough that the case against polygyny is rather weak. Even the Pharisees didn't ask whether adding wives was lawful. Remember, Jesus said he didn't come to abolish the law (Matt. 5:17–19), and even critics of polygyny admit it was lawful in the Old Testament. The Pharisees were simply hard-hearted when it came to divorce, since God had already gone on record about how he felt about men who divorced their wives and married other women (Mal. 2:16). This is why Moses, not God, reluctantly put in a clause for divorce. Christians who uphold all Old Testament Law (called reconstructionists) lose all credibility, since nearly all of them state that polygyny was unlawful under God's law; to believe such an outlandish doctrine, they must ignore several case laws in scripture.

No one is without error on this topic, since even some supporters of polygyny make the mistake of citing Exodus 21:10; however, as we will see in a later chapter, this verse refers to female slaves (concubines). We know polygyny is lawful because God not only had no law forbidding it, but he also had certain regulations for it, proving its lawfulness. One such regulation is in Leviticus 18:18. "Neither shalt thou take a wife to her sister, to vex her, to uncover her nakedness, beside the other in her life time."

Another error supporters of polygyny make is to cite Leviticus 18:18 to condemn sororal polygyny (cowives who are sisters); in reality, this isn't a blanket statement on sororal polygyny. When comparing scripture with scripture, it is qualified. Ezekiel 23:1–4 says,

> The word of the Lord came again unto me, saying, Son of man, there were two women, the daughters of one mother: And they committed whoredoms in Egypt; they committed whoredoms in their youth: there were their breasts pressed, and there they bruised the teats of their virginity. And the names of them were Aholah the elder, and Aholibah her sister: and they were mine, and they bare sons and daughters. Thus were their names; Samaria is Aholah, and Jerusalem Aholibah.

We can obviously conclude that God wouldn't portray himself as spiritually married to two sisters (also in Jer. 3:6–10) if it were a sin, so we must find out what Leviticus 18:18 means when it mentions "to vex her." The Hebrew word for "vex" is *tsarar*, which means "to oppress, distress, or enemy"; this regulation on sororal polygyny (a man marrying two sisters) is wrong only if the husband has the intent to marry her sister with cruel intentions to his current wife. This explains why God could portray himself as married to two sisters, and it also means men who are in a sororal marriage, whether in ancient Israel or today, aren't committing any sin. Scripture protected inheritance rights for children of polygynous marriages.

Deuteronomy 21:15–17 says,

> If a man have two wives, one beloved, and another hated, and they have born him children, both the beloved and the hated; and if the firstborn son be hers that was hated: Then it shall be, when he maketh his sons to inherit that which he hath, that he may not make the son of the beloved firstborn before the son of the hated, which is indeed the firstborn. But he shall acknowledge the son of the hated for the firstborn, by giving him a double portion of all that he hath: for he is the beginning of his strength; the right of the firstborn is his.

How can such a law exist if a man cannot have more than one wife? Then there is the Levite marriage vow in Deuteronomy 25:5–10:

> If brethren dwell together, and one of them die, and have no child, the wife of the dead shall not marry without unto a stranger: her husband's brother shall go in unto her, and take her to him to wife, and perform the duty of an husband's brother unto her. And it shall be, that the firstborn which she beareth shall succeed in the name of his brother which is dead, that his name be not put out of Israel. And if the man like not to take his brother's wife, then let his brother's wife go up to the gate unto the elders, and say, My husband's brother refuseth to raise up unto his brother a name in Israel, he will not perform the duty of my husband's brother. Then the elders of his city shall call him, and speak unto him: and if he stand to it, and say, I like not to take her; Then shall his brother's wife come unto him in the presence of the elders, and loose his shoe from off his foot, and spit in his

face, and shall answer and say, So shall it be done unto that man that will not build up his brother's house. And his name shall be called in Israel, The house of him that hath his shoe loosed.

The Levite marriage vow would go into effect whether a man was married or single. It also didn't matter whether a man was married or single, for Exodus 22:16–17 says, "And if a man entice a maid that is not betrothed, and lie with her, he shall surely endow her to be his wife. If her father utterly refuse to give her unto him, he shall pay money according to the dowry of virgins." Deuteronomy 24:5 says, "When a man hath taken a new wife, he shall not go out to war, neither shall he be charged with any business: but he shall be free at home one year, and shall cheer up his wife which he hath taken."

The case for polygyny is overwhelming; all these regulations are sufficient proof for anyone looking for honest answers. Common sense dictates that if you wanted to go into the food industry, you wouldn't ask whether it's legal. The fact that the FDA, USDA, and OSHA regulate the food industry is proof enough that it's legal within the government's regulations. Probably the most famous proof text used to support a monogamy-only view of God's law is Deuteronomy 17:16–17:

> But he shall not multiply horses to himself, nor cause
> the people to return to Egypt, to the end that he should
> multiply horses: forasmuch as the Lord hath said unto you,
> Ye shall henceforth return no more that way. Neither shall
> he multiply wives to himself, that his heart turn not away:
> neither shall he greatly multiply to himself silver and gold.

The first truth to know about these verses is that they are directed at the king of Israel (v. 14), not at the commoners. The critics of polygyny who cite these verses fail to state that a king should have only one horse or piece of gold and silver in addition to one wife. But the critics cannot have it both ways; the reality is that God condemns greed, which is a sin.

Adultery, Polygyny, and Divorce

He didn't want a king to trust in his own strength (horses) or in his riches (gold, silver); and he didn't want foreign wives to turn his heart.

The Israelites were forbidden from marrying certain foreign women (Deut. 7:3), but it was only certain nations at certain times (Num. 31:18; Deut. 20:14). The stories of both Ruth and Rahab prove that God was against unconverted foreign wives, not those who were converted.

> But king Solomon loved many strange women, together with the daughter of Pharaoh, women of the Moabites, Ammonites, Edomites, Zidonians, and Hittites; Of the nations concerning which the Lord said unto the children of Israel, Ye shall not go in to them, neither shall they come in unto you: for surely they will turn away your heart after their gods: Solomon clave unto these in love. And he had seven hundred wives, princesses, and three hundred concubines: and his wives turned away his heart. For it came to pass, when Solomon was old, that his wives turned away his heart after other gods: and his heart was not perfect with the Lord his God, as was the heart of David his father. For Solomon went after Ashtoreth the goddess of the Zidonians, and after Milcom the abomination of the Ammonites. And Solomon did evil in the sight of the Lord, and went not fully after the Lord, as did David his father. Then did Solomon build an high place for Chemosh, the abomination of Moab, in the hill that is before Jerusalem, and for Molech, the abomination of the children of Ammon. And likewise did he for all his strange wives, which burnt incense and sacrificed unto their gods. (1 Kings 11:1–8)

Solomon didn't follow God's law established for kings in Deuteronomy, and this led to his downfall. His fall came from his foreign or strange wives, which he'd multiplied. If Solomon had wives who were already converted, God would have had no issue with him, seeing that it was impossible for a believing wife to turn his heart and sacrifice to another god. So the reality is that using Deuteronomy 17:17 to condemn polygyny is rather silly. While ignoring the verses that regulated the practice of polygyny and also staying silent on Deuteronomy 17:17, which deals with hoarding and mentions only the prohibition on multiplying wives, critics expose themselves not as serious students of the Word. One wonders whether the critics own only one car, computer, TV, silver coin, gold coin, or piece of jewelry to abide by their interpretation of this law.

The covetous will not inherit the kingdom of God (1 Cor. 6:10); the Greek word for "covetous," *pleonektes*, means "desiring more or being eager for gain." So if one wishes to stick to the strict interpretation, one can have only a single item of anything. One thing is for sure: you can't say you can have only one wife but multiple possessions and use Deuteronomy 17:17 as a case law against polygyny. The monogamous-only crowd must insist that every polygynous man was in reality only an unbeliever. David, Gideon, and other men are barred from the kingdom of God. Then, based on a strict reading of Deuteronomy 17:17, Christians who own multiple material goods cannot enter the kingdom of God either. In the much-maligned Matthew 19:5, where Jesus said, "For this cause shall a man leave father and mother, and shall cleave to his wife," the Greek word for "wife," *gune*, can also mean wives (singular or plural), so it's perfectly within reason to believe that Jesus also said a man cleaves to his wives. The same is also true for Genesis 2:24; the Hebrew word *ishshah* can also be singular or plural; it is the critics of polygyny who fail to understand scriptural nuance.

There is no conflict with one man being "one" with two wives, since the Word of God clearly states that the man is the head of his household (Eph. 5:22). Jesus also told his parable of the ten virgins.

> Then shall the kingdom of heaven be likened unto ten virgins, which took their lamps, and went forth to meet the bridegroom. And five of them were wise, and five were foolish. They that were foolish took their lamps, and took no oil with them: But the wise took oil in their vessels with their lamps. While the bridegroom tarried, they all slumbered and slept. And at midnight there was a cry made, Behold, the bridegroom cometh; go ye out to meet him. Then all those virgins arose, and trimmed their lamps. And the

foolish said unto the wise, Give us of your oil; for our lamps are gone out. But the wise answered, saying, Not so; lest there be not enough for us and you: but go ye rather to them that sell, and buy for yourselves. And while they went to buy, the bridegroom came; and they that were ready went in with him to the marriage: and the door was shut. Afterward came also the other virgins, saying, Lord, Lord, open to us. But he answered and said, Verily I say unto you, I know you not. Watch therefore, for ye know neither the day nor the hour wherein the Son of man cometh. (Matt. 25:1–13)

The monogamy-only crowd state that the bridegroom will marry only one bride and that the other nine virgins are simply bridesmaids. However, this view runs into several problems. A marriage denotes an intimate relationship, which is why the *ecclesia*, the family of God, is portrayed as a bride waiting for Christ. We can conclude that the brides are believers, but who do the bridesmaids represent if there is only one bride? The bridegroom would come to take away the bride, not the bridesmaids. If the bridegroom marries only one wise virgin and leaves the other four wise virgins behind after the wedding, then Jesus won't have an intimate relationship with most Christians. So why would they be called "wise"? What is the point of the parable if the bridegroom ultimately leaves four of the five wise virgins behind? Ultimately, we should be married with Christ forever as a bride is married to her groom, not used for a day like a bridesmaid; thus, the plain reading of scripture tells us this is indeed a polygynous marriage, in which all five virgins marry the one bridegroom, and the foolish are left behind.

The context also testifies of this reality. In the previous chapter (24), Jesus warned that believers should be prepared for his return; then he mentioned the parable of the ten virgins, ten talents, sheep, and goats; it is utterly ridiculous to interpret that four of the five wise virgins simply participate in a monogamous marriage. These parables present an all-or-nothing view; either someone was with Jesus, such as the servants who used their talents wisely or sheep who were his. But with the ten virgins we don't have an all-or-nothing view? With this flawed exegesis, we have five who are foolish and won't be with Jesus. One is wise and will be married to him forever, but four wise virgins are neither explicitly shut out nor joined with him forever; they are simply in limbo. Even the Greek word for "virgin" is a special word denoting a "young virgin of marriageable age." Jesus would be saying, in essence, to "be prepared to not be joined with me forever." The very idea of bridesmaids is anachronistic in terms of Hebrew custom, and there is no biblical basis for it. Critics of polygyny must acknowledge that as believers we all have a personal relationship with Christ, so spiritually he is married to a great multitude. No other interpretation makes sense. Truth is like the tide of an ocean; you can fight against it, but you cannot prevail, no matter how hard you try.

A common argument for a monogamy-only view of scripture is to appeal to the creation story. God created only Eve for Adam, so this is proof of God's ideal for mankind, which is monogamy. This story doesn't prove monogamy is God's ideal; it proves only that the creation story is a special case. Should men marry prostitutes because God commanded Hosea to do so (Hos. 1:2)? Of course, no one would agree to such a statement; Hosea, like Adam and others throughout scripture, is a special case. Hosea didn't have the choice to marry a virgin, and Adam didn't have the choice of being celibate. One could make the following arguments from the creation story, in addition to the monogamy-only view:

1. We should be nude at all times.
2. We shouldn't eat any meat.
3. We should wait for God to bring us a spouse.
4. We should all be married.

If critics can't convince people through the creation story, then they resort to other fallacious arguments. Genesis 4:19–24 says,

> And Lamech took unto him two wives: the name of the one was Adah, and the name of the other Zillah. And Adah bare Jabal: he was the father of such as dwell in tents, and of such as have cattle. And his

> brother's name was Jubal: he was the father of all such as handle the harp and organ. And Zillah, she also bare Tubalcain, an instructer of every artificer in brass and iron: and the sister of Tubalcain was Naamah. And Lamech said unto his wives, Adah and Zillah, Hear my voice; ye wives of Lamech, hearken unto my speech: for I have slain a man to my wounding, and a young man to my hurt. If Cain shall be avenged sevenfold, truly Lamech seventy and sevenfold.

The argument is that because Lamech was a killer and polygynist, polygyny is a sin. It doesn't take much thought to refute this guilt-by-association fallacy. Lamech's being a killer has no bearing on polygyny whatsoever; besides, there are plenty of monogamist killers out there. One of Israel's most wicked kings was none other than King Ahab, and he was in a monogamous marriage with Jezebel. Does this mean monogamy is evil?

Throughout scripture we see examples that appear to condemn polygyny, but on closer examination, this isn't the case. Isaac and Rebekah, for example, were grieved because Esau married two Hittite women (Gen. 26:34), not because he married more than one woman. Jacob married Leah after working off the dowry for seven years, thinking she was Rachel (Gen. 29:23); he ended up working seven more years for Rachel (Gen. 29:29). Despite his two wives, who were sisters no less, God blessed Jacob and changed his name to Israel. He said he would give him the land he'd promised Abraham and Isaac. Apparently, God could tell him that a nation of kings would come from his loins (Gen. 35:11) but not that he should separate from Rachel and his concubines. Gideon, a man of God and of great faith, had many wives (Judg. 8:30) and wasn't condemned.

Samuel's father, Elkanah, had two wives, Peninnah and Hannah (1 Sam. 1:2). Hannah was barren but prayed to God for a son. God answered her prayers, and the result was one of Israel's greatest prophets—Samuel (1 Sam. 1:20). Why would God bless Hannah with a child if she was in a sinful polygynous relationship?

David won Saul's contest for his daughter, Michal, by bringing in the most foreskins and married her (1 Sam. 18:27); several years later David had at least six more wives: Ahinoam, Abigail, Maach, Haggith, Shephatiah, and Eglah (2 Sam. 3:2–5). God finally established David as king over Israel, and he took more wives (2 Sam. 5:12–13). As mentioned earlier in chapter 1, David walked on the roof of his house and saw Bathsheba washing herself; after finding out she was married to Uriah, he committed adultery with her. When he discovered she was pregnant, he tried to cover up the affair by having Uriah sleep with her. When that plot failed, he had Uriah murdered. God sent the prophet Nathan to David to convict him of his sins. He began by telling David that God had given him Saul's wives or women. Despite the fact that David already had several wives, God told him that he would have given him more (2 Sam. 12:8). The scriptures declare that the goodness of God leads to repentance (Rom. 2:4). Why, then, didn't God mention the fact that David should be only with Michal and that living with the others was sinful? This obviously would have been the perfect time to do so, but apparently God could condemn David for adultery and murder but not for polygyny, even though he supposedly hated it.

Amazingly, some Christians hate polygyny and the scriptural implications so much that they insist God gave Saul's wives to David so he could simply take care of them; however, this belief has two problems. First, God said he'd delivered Saul's wives into his bosom, which denotes an intimate relationship. Second, even if you reject the fact that "bosom" denotes intimacy, one cannot deny that David had sex with these women because the Bible mentions some of the children he had with them. So the critics are still left with the problem that God condemned David for the murder of Uriah and adultery with Bathsheba but not for having sex with any of Saul's former wives or concubines—not to mention the other wives he'd had sex with before he even inherited any of Saul's.

The fact remains that if there were an ideal time in scripture to condemn polygyny, this would have been it. The critics must also deal with the fact that Paul explicitly said adulterers won't inherit the kingdom of God (1 Cor. 6:9), but polygynists are mentioned in the "hall of faith" (Heb. 11:21, 32). In and of themselves, Solomon's seven hundred wives and three hundred concubines didn't lead to his downfall. The fact that he married strange (pagan) women is the sole culprit (1 Kings 11:1–13). God's anger was kindled against Solomon because he built an altar to their foreign gods and worshipped them; his numerous wives and concubines didn't anger God per se.

Rehoboam had eighteen wives and was made strong for three years; he dealt wisely and dispersed his children throughout Judah and Benjamin (2 Chron. 11:17–23). Abijah married a total of fourteen wives (2 Chron. 13:21). Josiah, who did right in the sight of the Lord, married two women who were given to him at the same time—by the high priest Jehoiada, no less (2 Chron. 24:2–3).

As was stated earlier in the introduction, Jesus didn't come to abolish the law; hence, polygyny today isn't sin, given the fact that God regulated it under the law. Here's another fact your pastor has probably never told you regarding polygyny: many may view these truths as politically incorrect; nevertheless, they are scripturally correct facts.

First Corinthians 7:2 says, "Nevertheless, to avoid fornication, let every man have his own wife, and let every woman have her own husband." The Greek word for "his own" is *heautou*, which means "possessive," while the Greek word for "her own," *idios*, is used as "being possessed" or "belonging to." Sound hermeneutics dictate that the wife belongs to her husband in the same sense that a servant belongs to his or her master.

Romans 14:4 says, "Who art thou that judgest another man's servant? to his own [*heautou*] master he standeth or falleth. Yea, he shall be holden up: for God is able to make him stand." The Greek word for "own" in this verse is the same word Paul used in 1 Corinthians 7:2 for a woman belonging to her husband; he could have easily used the same word, *heautou*, for husbands and wives, but he didn't. So much for the "men and women are equal" slogan so many Christians parrot; they apparently do so without a proper reading of scripture.

Ask why your pastors, who are presumably trained in the Greek language, don't point out this information. Another scripture Christians like to point out is 1 Timothy 3:2, 12). "A bishop then must be blameless, the husband of one wife, vigilant, sober, of good behaviour, given to hospitality, apt to teach...Let the deacons be the husbands of one wife, ruling their children and their own houses well."

These verses are often appealed to because they speak of a man who desires to be an overseer or deacon. He must be the husband of one wife. Even if one were to take these verses at face value, the verses would forbid polygyny only to those who desire a leadership position. There would be no need to point out that these positions are reserved only for monogamists if polygyny is a sin; it would be redundant to point this out unless polygyny isn't a sin and men not in leadership positions can still practice it. The fact is that Paul spoke to Timothy about the requirements for those desiring to be a deacon or overseer. He didn't state requirements for Christians in general, even though the word "deacon" is a transliterated word for "servant" and is used to describe an office in the *ecclesia*. Unless one wants to insist that all Christians must be married, this argument must be dropped. Besides, Jesus said that "some men are made eunuchs and other men are eunuchs for the Kingdom of Heaven's sake" (Matt. 19:12).

Here's another angle so many Christians—especially ones who think polygyny is biblical—overlook. If you were a business owner and needed to fill a job position, you would list the minimum requirements for filling the position. You wouldn't list that applicants require a GED, a high-school diploma, as well as associate's, bachelor's, master's, and doctorate degrees. You also wouldn't say that a prospective employee needs to be a young adult, one who is middle aged, or a senior citizen. You would simply state that the applicant should be at least eighteen years old and have at least a GED; no experience is necessary. This is true for any job opening; the bare minimum required is listed, and no one ever lists credentials that exceed the minimum. Paul's writing to Timothy was no different and listed the bare minimum requirements for each office, which is that a man should have at least one wife. To lead the *ecclesia*, one should at least have his own family to lead as an example.

Mia, the Greek word from the Timothy passages translated "one," can also be translated as "first" (Matt. 28:1) or "a" (Matt. 21:19). So Paul could very easily have said "husband of a wife" or "husband of first wife." The problem with interpreting *mia* as "first" is that divorcing and remarrying for any reason is adultery, regardless of whether one is in a leadership position; this issue will be detailed in the next chapter. Another issue with the "first" interpretation is that it would bar men who are widowed and remarried, but that doesn't make sense either, given the fact that marriage is for life and that death means you're free to remarry (Rom. 7:2). Still, if one were to stick to the "first" translation, it cannot be used to condemn polygyny as long as he is still with his first wife. This is no different from God's anger at the priest who dealt treacherously with the wife of his youth, which would be his first wife (Mal. 2:14–16). The biggest problem with the "one" interpretation is that the Greek word for the number one is *heis*. If Paul had wanted to forbid polygyny, there is little doubt that he would have used *heis*. We have already seen that Paul used *heautou* for husbands having their own wife, but he used *idios* to denote a wife belonging to her husband much like a servant belonged to his or her master (Rom. 14:4). So it's clear Paul didn't restrict husbands to only one wife. Paul used the word *heis* for "one" when he spoke of the qualifications (again notice the bare minimum requirements) of the *ecclesia* supporting a widow. First Timothy 5:9 says, "Let not a widow be taken into the number under threescore years old, having been the wife of one man." She should be at least sixty years old and be the wife of one man or husband.

Why did Paul use *heis* instead of *mia*? It should be obvious that Paul used *heis* in 1 Timothy 5:9 because a wife can have only one husband at a time. Hence, a woman who was sixty-one when her husband died could get support from the *ecclesia*, but a woman who was twice widowed and was sixty-six years old couldn't? Does this make any sense? Paul said "one" (*heis*) because that is all the law allowed: a woman can have only one husband at a time; anything else is adultery. When Paul used the word *mia* in 1 Timothy (3:2, 12), he didn't mean "one" or "first" as God's law allows only one husband at a time for wives but allows husbands to have many wives.

Also, if Paul had wanted to be clear on the translation of *mia* as "first," he could have cleared up all confusion by simply using the Greek word for "first," which is *protos*. The only alternative that makes sense is "husband of a wife," but even if all the preceding information wasn't enough to convince anyone (any reasonable-minded person should be convinced by now), this doesn't change the fact that Paul listed the minimum requirements for leadership in the *ecclesia*. Even if one were stubborn enough to say the requirement should be "husband of one wife," it could mean only that a deacon or overseer should have at least one wife and not be limited to one.

People who think polygyny is biblical make one common mistake: that a husband can add wives only if his previous wife or wives agree. A husband, as master of his own family, doesn't have to seek permission from any of his wives. The English word *husband* comes from the Middle English word *husbonde*, meaning "master of a house." Indeed, a man could ask for his wife's permission, but he isn't required to do so. The fact is that antipolygynist attitudes came mostly from the Roman Empire, and since a large number of Christians were inside the Roman Empire, they slowly adopted an antipolygynist view. It's no mistake that in many countries today, polygyny is legally recognized, and there are Christian polygynists.

There's no reason for people who profess to be Christians to treat polygynists as sinners or to discriminate against them in any way. Many Christians in the Western world look down on polygyny, but they do so without any biblical evidence whatsoever, as we have just seen. The fact is, polygyny is biblically based, and God blessed some of his faithful servants by giving them many wives. Many professing Christians in the West claim a biblical worldview, yet they attack and demean polygyny. The reality is that they have a secular or partial worldview and have just decided to adopt certain things they like from the Bible.

One last point critics of polygyny make is that a man cannot have multiple wives if the practice is illegal in the country in which he resides. Government doesn't need to recognize a marriage for it to be valid. There isn't one verse in the entire Bible that says the state must sanction a marriage, nor does one need a ceremony, as Isaac and Rebekah demonstrated. The same people who believe the government must sanction a marriage never state that the same logic must mean that a collapse of government dissolves all marriages for those the state married. While they state anyone must get the government's permission to get married, they continue to state that Adam and Eve were married. It could be said that Adam and Eve were the first ones who didn't need a ceremony or permission from any government, because none such existed yet. However, by the time Isaac married Rebekah by simply taking her into Sarah's tent (Gen. 24:67), there had been plenty of ceremonies, and some pagan nations recognized marriages.

Jesus was clear when he said his kingdom was "not of this world" (John 18:36). As Christians we are born from above. Likewise, a government that legalizes homosexual marriages doesn't make it legitimate to God. A lot of people reading this may say, "So polygyny might not be a sin, but the issue isn't really important." Actually, it *is* important because there are a lot of Christian missionaries who hold a false view regarding polygyny. When they go to countries and proselytize polygynist men, they make them divorce all their wives, save for the first, thereby destroying families and causing adultery, since some of the wives remarry. Trying to have it both ways, some missionaries say a polygynist shouldn't divorce his wives but cannot marry any additional women. But either polygyny is a sin, and a man should divorce all but his first wife, or it isn't a sin, and he can marry additional women if he chooses to.

Regardless of their intentions, missionaries who teach this false doctrine will be held accountable (James 3:1). Much like the Pharisees, they shut the way for many to enter the kingdom of God (Matt. 23:13). People who hold the incorrect view that monogamy isn't just the ideal but the *only* legitimate way to marry dominate Christianity. As Paul would say, they are "forbidding to marry" (1 Tim. 4:3). All a couple needs to get married is a commitment from both parties, since a marriage is a vow for life, and God holds us accountable for all our vows (Num. 30:2).

CHAPTER 3

Divorce + Remarriage = Adultery

WE NOW TURN OUR ATTENTION to one of the most egregious and common sexual sins, which is adultery through remarriage. Some Christians are shocked by the fact that various studies have shown that the Christian divorce rate is slightly higher than that of unbelievers. Most Christians believe someone can biblically divorce but only for adultery and abandonment; others believe someone can also divorce for verbal, emotional, physical, sexual, and financial abuse. Still others give a plethora of additional reasons why Christians can biblically get divorced and marry someone else. Some say divorce itself is a sin; others say someone can divorce but can't remarry. We will examine this issue in great detail, seeing that divorce is so widespread among professing Christians. In this current age, it isn't uncommon for people to call polygyny evil and immoral yet call divorce and remarriage in some or any circumstances good.

Unfortunately, many Christians don't properly meditate on the Word of God, but they call good evil and evil good (Isa. 5:20). Marriage is when a man and a woman (or women) make a commitment to be together for life. Marriage isn't just people dating or "shacking up"; it's a lifelong commitment God recognizes and joins together as marriage. Once this is done, the man and woman or women become one in an indissoluble bond that ends only at death. This view of marriage has weakened over time to the point that the divorce and remarriage of Christians are no big deal. There was a time when believers shunned and excommunicated divorced Christians who remarried, but that time is no more.

So what is the root of these problems? How did we get to this point? The discussion starts off with what many people coin the "exception clause," found in Matthew 19:9: "And I say unto you, Whosoever shall put away his wife, except it be for fornication, and shall marry another, committeth adultery: and whoso marrieth her which is put away doth commit adultery."

Once again we witness the peephole method, since critics rarely cite the "and whoso marrieth her which is put away doth commit adultery." Let's remove the peephole and cite Jesus's teaching on divorce and remarriage in its entirety.

> [3] The Pharisees also came unto him, tempting him, and saying unto him, Is it lawful for a man to put away his wife for every cause? [4] And he answered and said unto them, Have ye not read, that he which made them at the beginning made them male and female, [5] And said, For this cause shall a man leave father and mother, and shall cleave to his wife: and they twain shall be one flesh? [6] Wherefore they are no more twain, but one flesh. What therefore God hath joined together, let not man put asunder. [7] They say unto him, Why did Moses then command to give a writing of divorcement, and to put her away? [8] He saith unto them, Moses because of the hardness of your hearts suffered you to put away your wives: but from the beginning it was not so. [9] And I say unto you, Whosoever shall put away his wife, except it be for fornication, and shall marry another, committeth adultery: and whoso marrieth her which is put away doth commit adultery. [10] His disciples say unto him, If the case of the man be so with his wife, it is not good to marry. [11] But he said unto them, All men cannot receive this saying, save they to whom it is given. [12] For there are some eunuchs, which were so born from their mother's womb: and there are some eunuchs, which were made eunuchs of men: and there be eunuchs, which have made themselves eunuchs for the kingdom of heaven's sake. He that is able to receive it, let him receive it. (Matt. 19:3–12)

Divorce + Remarriage = Adultery

The first mistake many people make—even the ones who rightly state that divorce and remarriage are wrong—is misunderstanding the question. Can a man divorce his wife for any (the Greek word *pas* can be translated "any") reason (the Greek word *aitia* can be translated "reason")? Tempting Jesus, the Pharisees asked whether a man could divorce his wife for any reason. This is a crucial point because the traditional view is that the Pharisees asked whether a man could divorce his wife and marry another woman for any reason at all, or for a limited one. This misunderstanding of the question sets up a false paradigm that God sanctioned divorce and remarriage in some or all circumstances, and that remarriage is a sin depending only on the reason for the divorce.

In verse 4 Jesus answered the Pharisees' question concerning divorce for any reason, and it was an emphatic no! In verses 5–6, Jesus continued to give his reason for the permanence of marriage and said no man could "put [it] asunder." At no time did Jesus waver. By verse 7 we come to one of the widespread misinterpretations of scripture. The Pharisees asked Jesus why Moses had allowed a man to divorce his wife; nowhere did the Pharisees state that God allowed divorce. Jesus also stated that Moses, not God, permitted them to put away their wives. This was a decree from Moses God never endorsed; Jesus corrected that. Yet, to this day, some professing Christians insist that God, not Moses, allowed divorce. Clearly, Jesus disagreed with them when he said divorce was a Mosaic allowance (Deut. 24:1–4) in verse 8, but this is almost always overlooked.

> When a man hath taken a wife, and married her, and it come to pass that she find no favour in his eyes, because he hath found some uncleanness in her: then let him write her a bill of divorcement, and give it in her hand, and send her out of his house. And when she is departed out of his house, she may go and be another man's wife. And if the latter husband hate her, and write her a bill of divorcement, and giveth it in her hand, and sendeth her out of his house; or if the latter husband die, which took her to be his wife; Her former husband, which sent her away, may not take her again

to be his wife, after that she is defiled; for that is abomination before the Lord: and thou shalt not cause the land to sin, which the Lord thy God giveth thee for an inheritance. (Deut. 24:1–4)

There are several problems with appealing to the Mosaic allowance for divorce. First, only the husband, not the wife, could initiate the divorce. Second, the Hebrew word for "uncleanness," *ervah*, can also be defined as "nakedness, blemish, disgrace or indecency," which cannot be limited to sex. Such a broad range indicates that the Mosaic allowance enabled a man to divorce his wife for any reason. The Septuagint, which is the Greek version of the Old Testament, backs this up and uses the phrase "unbecoming thing" from the Greek word *aschemon*, which can also mean "inelegant or uncomely" (1 Cor. 12:23). Third, as has been previously mentioned, God didn't authorize any divorce; it was an allowance from Moses; hence, the name "Mosaic allowance." Fourth, Moses reluctantly permitted divorce; it wasn't a command for them to do so. Fifth, when anyone divorces with the intent to remarry, he or she exhibits hard-heartedness and unforgiveness.

Let's go back to Matthew 19:9. Jesus began the verse by saying, "And I say unto you." The word "and" is translated from the Greek word *de*, which can also mean "but," as some translations say. So when Jesus began verse 9, he, in fact, said, "but," which denotes a change from the previous verses, which in this case are verses 7–8. Also, the word "except" is translated from the Greek word *ei me*, which can also mean "if not" or "not," and the word "fornication" is translated from the Greek word *porneia*. In actuality, Jesus said, "But I say unto you, that whosoever shall put away his wife, not for fornication, and shall marry another, commits adultery; and he who marries one put away commits adultery." This is exactly how Matthew 19:9 reads in Darby's Translation, and there are several other translations that translate *ei me* as a negative adverb.

You're probably wondering whether such a conclusion can be drawn when the vast majority of translations translate *ei me* as "save for, except, unless" and so forth. As we shall see, all translations that do so end up contradicting themselves. There is only one true interpretation for Matthew

19:9; that it's the minority view among Christians and Bible translators doesn't change the fact that it's the correct view and the only one that makes sense.

Before we make the case for the proper interpretation of Matthew 19, we must examine the word "fornication," which is translated from the Greek word *porneia*. It is defined in the broadest terms as "illicit sex and spiritual adultery" (idolatry). Newer Bible versions translate *porneia* in terms that are broader than scripture allows, such as "marital unfaithfulness," "sexual immorality," and "immorality," while older versions use narrower terms, such as "prostitution," "whoredom," and "fornication." Immorality can include such sins as lying, impatience, and a quick temper; no one can make the argument that *porneia* includes such sins. It's no coincidence that as divorce rates increase, the newer Bible versions employ terms that are much broader.

Still, if one were to go with the broadest term possible, "immorality," and substitute it for "fornication" in Matthew 19:9 and ignore the fact that there's absolutely no basis whatsoever to define *porneia* as such, one is still left with a nonsensical teaching on divorce and remarriage. Matthew 19:9 says, "And I say unto you, Whosoever shall put away his wife, except it be for immorality, and shall marry another, committeth adultery: and whoso marrieth her which is put away doth commit adultery."

Let's say that Bill divorces his wife Marsha for immorality and later marries Suzy. Marsha, having been divorced from Bill, later marries Rick. If one believes someone can divorce and remarry for immorality, everything would appear to be fine, except for the fact that Jesus said, "And whoso marrieth her who is put away doth commit adultery." This means Rick commits adultery by marrying Marsha. It also means God still recognizes Bill as being married to Marsha, since there is no way Rick can commit adultery with Marsha if she is no longer married to Bill. It also logically follows that if Marsha is still married to Bill, even though he divorced her to marry Suzy, he is guilty of adultery per Mark 10:11–12. "And he saith unto them, Whosoever shall put away his wife, and marry another, committeth adultery against her. And if a woman shall put away her husband, and be married to another, she committeth adultery."

What *porneia* is defined as makes no difference—whether it's immorality, marital unfaithfulness, lying, stealing, or any type of abuse. Arguing about what *porneia* means or how it should be translated into English is really a red herring; what's important is that Christians who believe divorce and remarriage isn't (at least in all cases) a sin cannot make a logical argument for their doctrine. Many of the newer Bible versions omit the latter half of verse 9; there is no evidence to actually justify this omission. Most Greek manuscripts include this sentence, as do Matthew 5:32 and the prohibitions listed in Mark and Luke. While Christians who believe divorce and remarriage aren't always a sin differ as to what dissolves a marriage covenant, they all have at least one thing in common, and that's that someone can divorce for adultery. Matthew 19:9 says, "And I say unto you, Whosoever shall put away his wife, except it be for immorality, and shall marry another, committeth adultery."

Even when the latter half is deleted, one is left with a nonsensical conclusion. If Bill divorces Marsha for irreconcilable differences and marries Suzy, he commits adultery because the divorce isn't for immorality. Since Bill commits adultery by marrying Suzy, Marsha is free to remarry, since his adultery dissolved the marriage. It logically follows that if Marsha is free to remarry because she is no longer married to Bill, then he is no longer married to her, and his own adultery has freed him from his marriage. The end result is that Bill could get a divorce for any reason and dissolve the marriage because of the following:

1. A lawful divorce for immorality dissolves the marriage.
2. An unlawful divorce for anything that isn't immorality is sin leading to adultery.
3. Adultery is immorality and lawfully dissolves the marriage.

Some Christians try to avoid this obvious nonsensical outcome by insisting that only Marsha would be free to remarry if Bill divorced her for something other than immorality. But there isn't one single verse in scripture that even hints at such a conclusion. Don't we believe in *sola scriptura*? At no time does a marriage free one spouse to remarry and not the other. Either both are free to remarry, since the marriage has been dissolved, or the marriage cannot be dissolved, and Bill and Marsha are both guilty of adultery if they remarry following his divorce to her for irreconcilable differences.

So even when we use the broadest interpretation for *porneia* and completely delete Jesus's last sentence in Matthew 19:9, we're still left with a contradictory doctrine of divorce and remarriage, proving our point that such an allowance isn't scripturally and logically sound. Clearly, we can glean from Jesus's reply to the Pharisees in Matthew 19:4–8 that Jesus rejects divorce and remarriage; to say he turns around and says someone can in verse 9 is contradictory. Also, remember the latter half of verse 9, which states that anyone who marries a divorced woman commits adultery. Those who believe in divorce and remarriage have a schizophrenic Jesus, who says no in verses 4–8, yes in the first half of verse 9, and no in the latter half of verse 9.

Verse 10, where the disciples say, "It is not good to marry," would be further proof that Jesus didn't allow divorce and remarriage. By translating *ei me* as "not for," we harmonize Matthew 19:9 completely with the latter half of the verse along with verses 4–8, and we understand the disciples' shock at Jesus's teaching in verse 10. Anyone who still insists that divorce and remarriage is lawful has to admit that his or her doctrine isn't logically sound and that he or she is hard-hearted (v. 8). Jesus's teaching here was intended to clear up confusion in regard to divorce and remarriage; much like in his Sermon on the Mount, he wanted to clarify God's laws, which the Pharisees were misusing, since many mistakenly believed the Mosaic allowance was from God himself. Despite Jesus's clarification, there are still Christians who insist God allows divorce and remarriage; this, however, is one of the reasons why teachers of God's Word will receive a stricter judgment (James 3:1).

Let's return to Deuteronomy 24:4. The word for "former husband" is *ba'al*, meaning "master" or "lord," but the latter man is simply described as *iysh* (v. 1–3). Why the difference? The first is described as a husband or master; the second could just be called a man or husband. Because the second man is simply called *iysh* and not *ba'al*, we can glean that he isn't seen as the legitimate husband. Moses could have easily called the second man *ba'al*, much like he did the first husband; this is proof that *iysh* should be translated "man," not "husband." Moses says that if the second man hates her or dies, she cannot return to the first husband because she has been defiled (v. 4). Why is she defiled? It's obvious that she is defiled because she committed adultery by being with another man. Notice that she is defiled only when she has been with another man; if she were to stay single, it would be possible for her to go back to her husband. Also notice verse 4 says it's an abomination (the Hebrew word is *tow'ebah*) if she goes back to her husband after she has been defiled. This is because the sin of adultery is an abomination (*tow'ebah*) that defiles the land in Leviticus 18:27. When she "marries" another "husband," they should both be put to death for adultery; yet, the Mosaic allowance prevented this from happening. Moses prevented the divorced woman who had remarried from going back to her first husband so as not to compound the problem, seeing that she and her second "husband" shouldn't even be alive to begin with.

When Moses came up with his allowance for divorce, he knew God didn't recognize the ending of the marriages just because the wife had been given a bill of divorcement. There was never a time in Israel when a man could divorce his wife and marry another person, nor could a man marry a divorced woman. Doing so has always been, and always will be, adultery. God commanded the Israelites to love their neighbor as themselves (Lev. 19:18); this couldn't be obeyed if a man were to divorce his wife.

Many Christians who promote divorce and remarriage teach that adultery is only a single act and not a continual event. Let's return to the previous scenario. Let's say Bill divorces Marsha and marries Suzy. When Bill has sex with Suzy the first time, they say, he commits adultery, but he doesn't commit adultery for every subsequent event; the same would hold true for Rick when he marries Marsha. Once again we're left with a nonsensical outcome because Bill is guilty of adultery the first time he has sex but not thereafter. So the act that condemns Bill of adultery, the first time, simultaneously dissolves the marriage and saves him from adultery thereafter. When it comes to Christians who support divorce and remarriage, one thing they always assume is that the remarriage is valid, regardless of scriptural evidence to the contrary. Just to drive home the absurdity of this argument, imagine that Bill doesn't divorce Marsha, but she has an affair with Rick instead. Would this be adultery only the first time they have sex? Would anyone dare say that each subsequent time they have sex isn't adultery? Would anyone say that if they've had an affair for so many years, they can stay together? Of course, critics would be quick to say that Bill is still married to Marsha, so she and Rick must forsake their sin. But this is exactly the point proponents fail to see. God doesn't recognize divorce, so even if Bill divorces Marsha and she marries Rick, they are still committing adultery.

Many teachers and overseers in the *ecclesia* purport to hold a high view of scripture; they correctly teach that divorce and remarriage for any reason is adultery. Yet, they are quick to state that if a couple is divorced and remarried, they should stay in their current relationship because divorcing would compound the problem. There are several problems with this teaching, the first of which is the fact that at no time does Jesus give people who divorce and remarry (even if it's for immorality) permission to do so. Second, at no time does Jesus—or anyone for that matter—state there is a statute of limitations for adultery or any sin. How, then, could any teacher of the Word of God make such a bold statement?

The author has theorized that those who know the permanence of marriage is scriptural want it both ways. For many Christian ministers, depending on their geographic location, anywhere from 20 to 35 percent of their listening audience, congregation, and readers are divorced and remarried; in some areas the numbers may be even higher. By teaching that the remarried should stay in their present situation, these pastors won't lose any members or have to worry about taking a pay cut or losing their job altogether. These same pastors can also claim that they hold a high view of scripture by teaching that divorce and remarriage for any reason is adultery for everyone else. This way they lose only a few of their members, who choose to divorce, while keeping the vast majority, who are already remarried, and also accepting new members who are.

They claim to be conservative and hold to a high view of scripture, but actions always speak louder than words. Bill, who divorced Marsha and married Suzy, is asked to leave his nondenominational church after being a member for several years because he divorced and remarried. His pastor teaches the permanence of marriage in theory only because he allows those who are already divorced and remarried to stay in their current state. The obvious double standard upsets Bill, and he goes to another nondenominational church, where they also teach the permanence of marriage like Bill's old church, but since he is already remarried, he is told to stay in his current relationship to avoid compounding the problem.

Of course, this scenario is completely unlikely to happen only because most pastors don't even bother to teach the permanence of marriage, and they have all kinds of exceptions that can dissolve it. The author has provided this example just to show how even the most "conservative" teachers of the Word are, in fact, liberal on divorce and remarriage. Many of these pastors are interested only in their own filthy lucre. Some are just confused, which explains why they state that a divorced and remarried couple should stay in their current state. Yet, many of those same teachers know that divorce and remarriage for any reason is adultery. How can these "conservative" teachers say otherwise, unless it's for money or because they're confused? Nowhere does scripture say that if you've been divorced and remarried for several years, it's no longer an adulterous relationship. Nor does it make sense for any *ecclesia* to allow divorced and remarried people into their congregation while disallowing current members from divorcing.

After adultery the most common excuse for divorce and remarriage is abandonment, and proponents cite Paul in 1 Corinthians. One wonders why Jesus didn't mention this reason twenty years earlier when he walked the earth, since *porneia* doesn't mean desertion. Instead of reading 1 Corinthians 7:15 alone, let's remove the peephole and read Paul's words in context. First Corinthians 7:10–16 says,

> And unto the married I command, yet not I, but the Lord, Let not the wife depart from her husband: But and if she depart, let her remain unmarried, or be reconciled to her husband: and let not the husband put away his wife. But to the rest speak I, not the Lord: If any brother hath a wife that believeth not, and she be pleased to dwell with him, let him not put her away. And the woman which hath an husband that believeth not, and if he be pleased to dwell with her, let her not leave him. For the unbelieving husband is sanctified by the wife, and the unbelieving wife is sanctified by the husband: else were your children unclean; but now are they holy. But if the unbelieving depart, let him depart. A brother or a sister is not under bondage in such cases: but God hath called us to peace. For what knowest thou, O wife, whether thou shalt save thy husband? or how knowest thou, O man, whether thou shalt save thy wife?

Paul clearly said a wife shouldn't leave her husband, and if she does, she must not remarry, but she may reconcile with her husband (v. 10). So how can anyone draw the conclusion from verse 15 that she can remarry? Unfortunately, many modern translations, kowtowing to the divorced and remarried crowd, use "bound" instead of "bondage." You might ask why. Well, let's look at their motive. Romans 7:2–3 says,

> For the woman which hath an husband is bound by the law to her husband so long as he liveth; but if the husband be dead, she is loosed from the law of her husband. So then if, while her husband liveth, she be married to another man, she shall be called an adulteress: but if her husband be dead, she is free from that law; so that she is no adulteress, though she be married to another man.

Many want you to think that when a woman is deserted, she's no longer bound in the same sense as when a woman's husband dies; thus, a woman who is deserted is just as free to remarry as a widow. The problem is the Greek word *douloo* (1 Cor. 7:15), which is translated in the KJV as "under bondage" and means "enslaved" or "under subjection." Paul simply said an abandoned woman isn't under the bondage of marital duties because her husband has left her. At no time did Paul say or even imply that she is free to remarry—quite the contrary. In verse 11 he explicitly said she cannot. One important stumbling block proponents cannot get over is the fact that if Paul allowed the remarriage of a deserted woman, why didn't he give a minimum duration of what constitutes abandonment?

It's rather odd that countries that allow divorce for desertion always give qualifications that must be met, whether it's being abandoned two years or six months. Paul, who gave qualifications for deacons and overseers, didn't do so for abandonment. Apparently, according to proponents, the abandoned spouse can simply decide what constitutes abandonment, whether it's four hours, four days, or four years. Or maybe one of the "conservative" teachers of the scriptures gets to decide, but even they rarely, if at all, use a one-size-fits-all approach for the length of time one is abandoned before he or she can remarry. According to proponents of divorce and remarriage for abandonment, man's laws are actually higher than God's because man's laws require a set duration of time, while God requires none whatsoever.

When we read Paul's statements, we come to the following conclusions: A wife shouldn't depart her husband, but if she does, she must either reconcile with her husband or remain unmarried. A husband shouldn't depart from his wife. If a believer is married to an unbeliever and the unbeliever wants to stay, the believer shouldn't leave him or her. While Paul gave his own opinion on this particular matter, it didn't contradict what Jesus taught, because at no time did Paul say that a believer could depart from or divorce his or her spouse and remarry another person. If the unbelieving spouse chooses to leave the believer, the believer isn't required to render marital duties.

It's quite pathetic that those who support divorce and remarriage have to resort to slanted newer Bible versions. By translating *douloo* as "bound" instead of "under bondage," they give the impression that people are free to remarry because "bound" is used in Romans 7:2. However, "bound" in

Divorce + Remarriage = Adultery

Romans 7 is from the Greek word *deo*; these are two totally different words with different meanings. Even if Paul used *deo* in 1 Corinthians 7 instead of *douloo*, he still gave no permission to remarry and explicitly forbade it in verses 10–11. By appealing to Romans 7, proponents of divorce and remarriage actually defeat their own case. Romans 7:2–3 says,

> For the woman which hath an husband is bound by the law to her husband so long as he liveth; but if the husband be dead, she is loosed from the law of her husband. So then if, while her husband liveth, she be married to another man, she shall be called an adulteress: but if her husband be dead, she is free from that law; so that she is no adulteress, though she be married to another man.

Paul actually taught the permanence of marriage, which agrees with Jesus's teaching on the subject. While purposefully confusing *deo* with *douloo*, proponents fail to realize that Romans 7 doesn't endorse a woman to divorce and remarry for any reason, so their argument on this point is moot. Also, remember that the woman in Deuteronomy 24 was defiled when she married another man.

The desired result is justification for divorce and remarriage, which God hates and calls violence (Mal. 2:13–16). At one time those who were divorced and remarried weren't allowed in the *ecclesia*. Now, anyone who holds the correct view in regard to divorce and remarriage is in the minority. In 1 Corinthians 7:8–9, Paul said the unmarried and widowed can marry if they so choose. Proponents apply those verses to verse 11 and say a divorced woman can remarry. This is based on translating "unmarried" from the Greek word *agamos*, but once again context defeats this argument. The woman in verse 11 left her husband, so she was married, *gameo*, in Greek; the word for "unmarried" is *agamos*, which literally means "not married." Paul told a woman who had departed her husband not to marry but to be reconciled to her husband. To have Paul say the divorced woman is eligible to remarry in verses 8–9 and then turn around and contradict himself by saying she should be either unmarried or reconciled to her husband is nonsensical. Also, this "unmarried" woman (v. 11) has a husband just a few words later.

During the time the scriptures were written, there were no quotation marks we use today to denote something that doesn't actually occur. When Paul said a woman who departs her husband should reconcile with her husband or remain unmarried, she isn't truly unmarried, or Paul would have given remarriage as a third option. The same is true when Bill divorces Marsha and marries Suzy; he isn't really "married" to her because if he was, he wouldn't be committing adultery. So when Paul spoke of the unmarried (v. 8) being able to marry (v. 9), that doesn't mean he spoke of the same woman in verse 11; he couldn't have been speaking of the same woman given the command he gave her that didn't include remarrying.

When *porneia* is stretched to mean just about anything, true Christians shouldn't be surprised, though Jesus told the Pharisees that Moses had allowed them to divorce because they were hard-hearted; that is a trait of unbelievers. It's no surprise, then, that a good portion of professing Christians are hard-hearted and divorcing for any reason. Much like a crack in a ship, divorce was at first not allowed at all, and anyone who did it was shunned. Then cracks started to appear as people clamored to justify divorce for adultery, abandonment, pornography, physical and verbal abuse, impotence, physical and mental disabilities, and so forth. The fact is, this issue isn't about divorce for limited reasons, as they would have you believe, but for divorce for any reason. That is the real battle here.

This issue isn't about wanting to study God's Word but about people who profess to be Christian but have a secular worldview. They pick a few things they like from the Jesus buffet to paint themselves with a thin veneer of Christianity. If they were serious about God's Word, they wouldn't be saying someone can divorce and remarry for any reason. The reality is that when secular society began to allow divorce for limited circumstances, Christians began to adopt this view. So when secular society began allowing no-fault divorce, professing Christians followed suit once again.

The last major scripture proponents of divorce and remarriage appeal to in defending their beliefs is God's divorce from Israel in Jeremiah. But once again, when we look at everything in context, this passage actually weakens the case for divorce and remarriage. Jeremiah 3:1, 8, 14, and 20 says,

> They say, If a man put away his wife, and she go from him, and become another man's, shall he return unto her again? shall not that land be greatly polluted? but thou hast played the harlot with many lovers; yet return again to me, saith the Lord...And I saw, when for all the causes whereby backsliding Israel committed adultery I had put her away, and given her a bill of divorce...Turn, O backsliding children, saith the Lord; for I am married unto you: and I will take you one of a city, and two of a family, and I will bring you to Zion... Surely as a wife treacherously departeth from her husband, so have ye dealt treacherously with me, O house of Israel, saith the Lord.

In Jeremiah 3:1, God told Israel to come back to him despite his putting her away. This verse is further proof that God didn't write the divorce law found in Deuteronomy 24; God said, "They say," not "I said," and he called for his wife Israel to return to him. Verses 8 and 20 detail the fact that Israel actually committed adultery and abandoned him for other gods, yet this doesn't prove that God's divorce ended his marriage to Israel; in fact, it was quite the opposite. Once again the proponents' case is weak because God is still married to Israel despite his divorce. Israel's adultery doesn't free her to pursue other gods, and God didn't follow up his divorce by remarrying Egypt, Ethiopia, or any other nation. God's divorce of his wife Israel is in perfect sync with Paul's and Jesus's teaching on divorce; God sought to reconcile with his wife and didn't remarry. Most important, in verse 14 God said he was still married to Israel after he sent her a bill of divorcement (v. 8).

Some argue that God did, in fact, divorce Israel and remarry the *ecclesia*, but this isn't the case. One must remember that Abraham's descendants are of faith, not blood (Gal. 3:26–29). God didn't divorce Israel for the *ecclesia* because the *ecclesia* is Israel (Gal. 6:16). He is still married to

Israel; he just gave a better covenant to her. Besides, how can those who believe God divorced Israel and remarried the *ecclesia* explain Romans 11: 1–24? When Paul said some branches were broken off and that a wild branch was grafted in, he could have been referring only to Gentiles being added to the remnant, Israel. If one believes Israel and the *ecclesia* are two different entities, then what were the Gentiles grafted into?

Now that we've gone over the scriptures proponents of divorce and remarriage use, it's time to review scriptures that explicitly condemn the act of remarriage. These are scriptures proponents avoid. We've already shown that their best scriptures not only disprove their view when read in context but also prove the permanence of marriage. Malachi 2:13–16 says,

> And this have ye done again, covering the altar of the Lord with tears, with weeping, and with crying out, insomuch that he regardeth not the offering any more, or receiveth it with good will at your hand. Yet ye say, Wherefore? Because the Lord hath been witness between thee and the wife of thy youth, against whom thou hast dealt treacherously: yet is she thy companion, and the wife of thy covenant. And did not he make one? Yet had he the residue of the spirit. And wherefore one? That he might seek a godly seed. Therefore take heed to your spirit, and let none deal treacherously against the wife of his youth. For the Lord, the God of Israel, saith that he hateth putting away: for one covereth violence with his garment, saith the Lord of hosts: therefore take heed to your spirit, that ye deal not treacherously.

Rampant divorce is nothing new. During the time of Malachi, God spoke out against divorce and remarriage. He rebuked the Israelites for divorcing the wife of their youth and marrying younger women, and he called doing so treachery. Some critics assert this means divorce itself is sin; however, one must compare scripture with scripture. In 1 Corinthians 7:11, we read that a wife can depart from her spouse. The question isn't about divorce itself because if God did, in fact, recognize divorce, remarriage wouldn't be adultery; the question is what one does after the divorce takes place. This means the men God rebuked in Malachi simply didn't divorce their wives and stay single; they married new wives. That God calls their first wife the wife of their youth would seem to indicate that once they got older, the wives were put away for younger women. Nowhere does scripture state that divorce or separation itself constitutes sin, and if someone were to appeal to Malachi 2 as evidence for such, then he or she would run into a quandary because God divorced Israel in Jeremiah 3.

While he or she is correct in teaching the permanence of marriage, he or she fails to realize that divorce means nothing if marriage is an irrevocable covenant. This is why we can deduce that the men in Malachi divorced their wives and married new ones. In this one area, Christians who view divorce as sin believe similarly as those who approve of divorce and remarriage—that divorce can have an effect on marriage. Mark 10:1–12 says,

> And he arose from thence, and cometh into the coasts of Judaea by the farther side of Jordan: and the people resort unto him again; and, as he was wont, he taught them again. And the Pharisees came to him, and asked him, Is it lawful for a man to put away his wife? tempting him. And he answered and said unto them, What did Moses command you? And they said, Moses suffered to write a bill of divorcement, and to put her away. And Jesus answered and said unto them, For the hardness of your heart he wrote you this precept. But from the beginning of the creation God made them male and female. For this cause shall a man leave his father and mother, and cleave to his wife; And they twain shall be one flesh: so then they are no more twain, but one flesh. What therefore God hath joined together, let not man put asunder. And in the house his disciples asked him again of the same matter. And he saith unto them, Whosoever shall put away his wife, and marry another, committeth adultery against her. And if a woman shall put away her husband, and be married to another, she committeth adultery.

In Mark we read Jesus's teaching regarding divorce and remarriage without the exception clause, which states that you cannot divorce and remarry. What is interesting to note about Jesus's teaching in Mark is that a woman who divorces her husband and marries another man commits adultery. This was unheard of to the Israelites, since the Mosaic allowance didn't allow such a thing to take place. Luke 16:18 says, "Whosoever putteth away his wife, and marrieth another, committeth adultery: and whosoever marrieth her that is put away from her husband committeth adultery." Jesus's teaching on divorce and remarriage in Luke is the shortest, yet it is straight to the point and self-explanatory.

In a last desperate attempt to defend their beliefs, proponents of divorce and remarriage say God distinguishes between putting away and divorcing. "God hates putting away, not divorce," they say. "God was angry only because they weren't given the proper papers and were sent away empty handed." Well, let's go back through scripture and see whether putting away and divorce are unrelated to each other. First, we are still presented with a problem in Deuteronomy 24 because even if a wife is given a proper writ of divorce, she cannot go back to her first husband. Even if the second one dies, she is still defiled.

Returning once again to Matthew 19:9 and defining *porneia* in the broadest way imaginable to give divorce and remarriage proponents every advantage possible, we would still be left with a nonsensical conclusion. If we were to assume that "putting away" meant not giving a spouse proper paperwork or none at all, Jesus would be saying that a man can put away his wife, without any paperwork, for immorality, marry another woman, and not be guilty of adultery. This also means a man could divorce his wife for any reason, as long as he gave her a proper writ of divorcement. This also contradicts Matthew 19:3–8, where the Pharisees asked Jesus whether putting away a wife for any reason was lawful. So if Bill puts away his wife, Marsha (how can he do this without divorcing her?), and marries Suzy, how is he not committing adultery? If Rick marries Bill's put-away wife, how is Rick not committing adultery?

Why would the Pharisees ask Jesus whether someone can put away a wife for any reason if Jesus says someone can divorce for any reason as long as the proper paperwork is done? Were the Pharisees too lazy to get a writ of divorce and dissolve their marriages? In Malachi 2, is God angry because the Israelites were simply putting away their wives and not serving them papers of divorce? Would God have been happy (and have omitted this passage) if they'd simply given their wives a proper divorce? So when the Israelites put away the wives of their youth, that was treachery, but divorcing them isn't? Putting away is violence done to the family, but divorcing isn't? "From the beginning it was not so." What wasn't so?—putting away or divorcing? Why didn't Jesus just explicitly say to get a proper writ of divorce? Let's also not forget that Jesus condemned any man who married a divorced woman. It's quite evident that putting away and divorcing are not two different things.

Putting away and divorcing are interchangeable; God doesn't recognize divorce for any reason, so arguing about the meaning of words is a waste of time. Besides, we've already seen God put away Israel by giving her a bill of divorcement in Jeremiah. The Greek word for "put away" is *apuluo*, which means "release, loose, pardon, let go," and so forth. The Greek word for divorce is *apostasion*; while these words are different, they are used interchangeably. When one does *apostasion*, he or she releases, lets go, dismisses, and so forth, which is no different from *apuluo*.

Another favorite of the divorce and remarriage proponents is to say that if someone were divorced and remarried before becoming a believer, he or she can stay in his or her current state; or, if the person was divorced before being a believer, he or she can choose to remarry. It should be crystal clear by now that God doesn't recognize divorce at any time for any reason whatsoever. So if Bill divorces Marsha, marries Suzy, and becomes a believer years later, he must forsake his current "marriage" to be right with God. Proverbs 28:13 says, "He that covereth his sins shall not prosper: but whoso confesseth and forsaketh them shall have mercy."

A man who stole a car while being an unbeliever and now professes to be a believer must return the car; no one would tell him to keep it and just say, "I'm sorry." Likewise, if Rick married Marsha while he was an unbeliever, he cannot stay "married" to her after he professes to be a believer. He must forsake his sin; saying he's sorry before the congregation or pastor and then going to bed that night with Bill's wife isn't repentance. Sad to say, but repentance has become a lost art in Christianity today. Critics would say that a murderer cannot resurrect his or her victim, so someone who is divorced and remarried cannot resurrect his or her prior marriage. This is an apples-and-oranges comparison. First, the prior marriage isn't dead; if it was, then the remarriage wouldn't be adultery in the first place. Second, how does anyone know for certain that the spouse in the prior marriage won't reconcile? The only way we know for certain that a marriage cannot be reconciled is if the spouse is dead, but if this is the case, one is free to remarry. A murderer who repents cannot resurrect his or her victim, but the murderer can acknowledge that what he or she did was wrong and suffer the consequences. Bill should leave Suzy and pray for reconciliation with Marsha. If reconciliation never takes place, this is a consequence of his sin, and he must be a eunuch for the kingdom of heaven's sake.

If scripture allowed divorce for unbelievers, ignoring the general view against adultery in Leviticus 18:20–24, we would have one of the biggest loopholes imaginable. As every professing believer who wanted to divorce his or her spouse would claim, he or she wasn't a real believer when he or she divorced. The believer could also claim that his or her spouse is a believer but that the believer backslid when he or she got divorced; he or she is now a believer once more when he or she gets his or her new spouse. The fact is that God's laws are for believers and unbelievers; he isn't a respecter of persons (Acts 10:34).

In Ezra 9–10 and Nehemiah 13:23–25, we find examples of Israelites divorcing foreign women. While it's true that God forbade them from marrying foreign wives (Deut. 7:2–3), this doesn't mean the marriages they conducted were unlawful per se, because we don't know all the details of these marriages. If they divorced their wives to marry these foreign women, then they were correct to repent of these foreign remarriages. On the other hand, if there was no divorce involved (which is likely the case) and if the Israelites married these foreign wives, then the marriages were, in fact, lawful. When Esau married foreign wives, he grieved his parents, but they knew the marriages were lawful (Gen. 26:34–35). Even Jacob, who didn't marry foreign wives but a woman he didn't want, knew his being deceived didn't invalidate his marriage to Leah.

Ezra 10:2–4, 15–17 says,

> And Shechaniah the son of Jehiel, one of the sons of Elam, answered and said unto Ezra, We have trespassed against our God, and have taken strange wives of the people of the land: yet now there is hope in Israel concerning this thing. Now therefore let us make a covenant with our God to put away all the wives, and such as are born of them, according to the counsel of my lord, and of those that tremble at the commandment of our God; and let it be done according to the law. Arise; for this matter belongeth unto thee: we also will be with thee: be of good courage, and do it… Only Jonathan the son of Asahel and Jahaziah the son of Tikvah were employed about this matter: and Meshullam and Shabbethai the Levite helped them. And the children of the captivity did so. And Ezra the priest, with certain chief of the fathers, after the house of their fathers, and all of them by their names, were separated, and sat down in the first day of the tenth month to examine the matter. And they made an end with all the men that had taken strange wives by the first day of the first month.

Reading Ezra 10 reveals the following facts:

1. The priest Ezra wasn't even the one who came up with the idea for them to divorce their foreign wives; it's Shechaniah's idea.
2. They put away their wives and children according to the law. We know that the law in regard to divorce was from Moses, not God.
3. At no time did God tell Ezra to put away their wives.

4. Malachi, the last book written in the Old Testament, records God's utter hatred for divorce.
5. Ezra didn't tell them to marry new wives to replace their foreign ones.
6. Paul told Christians not to be unequally yoked with unbelievers (2 Cor. 6:14–15); doing so would have been the equivalent of an Israelite marrying a Canaanite. Yet, Paul said that if a believer did depart, he or she couldn't remarry (1 Cor. 7:11).
7. Why would God allow unbelief as a reason for divorce and remarriage in the Old Testament but not allow that reason in the New Testament?
8. Not everyone was in favor of this mass divorce, and while their motive cannot be ascertained, we should still note that there was opposition to this plan.
9. The investigations took time, so there is a good possibility that some of the converted foreign wives weren't divorced.

We won't go much further on either Ezra or Nehemiah, since sufficient evidence has been shown to refute the idea that God endorses divorce from these passages. In passing, we should note that Ruth and Rahab were foreign women, yet no one doubts they had converted their faith to that of the one true God (Ruth 1:15–16; Heb. 11:31). Nevertheless, nowhere does God employ a double standard for divorce in terms of a spouse's faith.

Divorce and remarriage are inconsistent with Christianity in general; when we've been wronged, we should forgive repeatedly. Jesus taught this in the parable of the unforgiving servant (Matt. 18:23–35). You cannot divorce your spouse and remarry and expect God to hear your prayers. God is not a respecter of persons; he treats us all equally, and his servants should do the same. Peter told us that "husbands should dwell with their wives and give them honor, so that their prayers be not hindered" (1 Pet. 3:7). Of course, forgiveness isn't just something that should be practiced between spouses; this is something every Christian must do. It's mind-boggling that some Christians correctly teach that we can't hold a grudge against a coworker because of the sin of unforgiveness, but they have no problem encouraging believers to divorce and remarry.

A common excuse people like to give is that divorced couples have forgiven each other and moved on. However, this cannot be the case because if they had really forgiven each other, they would be reconciled and living together as God expects a husband and wife to do. The audacity of people who divorce their spouse and marry someone else is completely unbelievable; they think God has forgiven them and that they will judge the world (including angels) with Christ (1 Cor. 6:1–3), while they have not done so for their spouse. Such thinking is absurd. Christians tolerate no other sin so much as divorce and remarriage; they probably tolerate it more than lying. Jesus said he will never leave us or forsake us (Heb. 13:5). He taught us repeatedly that we must forgive others (Matt. 6:14–15; 18:21–22; Mark 11:25). The Lord's Prayer is another example of the necessity of forgiveness. Jesus said, "Forgive us our debts, as we also have forgiven our debtors" (Matt. 6:12).

Jesus stated that not everyone who says, "Lord, Lord will enter into the Kingdom of Heaven only those that do the will of the Father" (Matt. 7:21). Those who work iniquity and profess to know him will be told that he never knew them (Matt. 7:23). The Greek word for "iniquity" is *anomia*, which means "illegality, violation of the law, and unrighteousness"; these are the people who think they have a relationship with God when in fact they don't. If you break God's law, you don't know him, so he doesn't know you. Similarly, Jesus says that if you deny him, he will deny you before the angels of God (Luke 12:9). People who profess to be Christians and are divorced and remarried would qualify as people God doesn't know because they transgress his laws, whether intentionally or unintentionally.

Remember that God is love (1 John 4:8); his love isn't conditional, because conditional love isn't love. So if we serve a God, who loved us first in spite of our faults—whether past, present, or future—how can someone say to his or her spouse, "I want a divorce" and later remarries? Is a servant greater than his master (John 13:16)? Whenever people divorce their spouse, they essentially say, "I love you as long as you make me happy."

The more "conservative" professing Christians will say, "I love you unless you commit adultery or become seriously ill or disabled."

This isn't real love; it's conditional, which in reality is self-love because they are happy only when they get what they want from their spouse. Many Christians are aghast when they hear of those who divorce their spouse when they are seriously ill or come into a large fortune or lose one. But marriage vows are "for better or worse, for rich or for poor, in sickness and in health." Why are some outraged when divorce happens for those reasons but not for adultery or abuse? Regardless of whether someone divorces someone else for adultery or poverty, the question we must ask is this: Did he or she really love his or her spouse to begin with? What most people call love is, in reality, self-gratification; this belief is now common among Christians. In reality love never fails (1 Cor. 13:8); this is the polar opposite of the conditional, shallow love of the world. Unconditional love thinks of others and what's best for them; it doesn't think about oneself.

You're probably wondering why all the scriptures regarding divorce and remarriage involve a total prohibition of divorced women from marrying, even if their husband runs off. Unfortunately, many Christians who correctly state it's adultery for the innocent woman to remarry make the mistake of inferring from scripture that it must be true for the innocent husband as well. The reason you can't make this inference is because, as we have seen, men and women have different roles, and the husband has authority over the wife. If a believer were to quit following Christ and serve another god, Christ wouldn't be barred from having more followers. Scripture provides us with an example when Michal went to be Phalti's "wife" (1 Sam. 25:44). During this time David still added wives but didn't commit adultery because he didn't put Michal away to marry his other wives; nor did he have to wait for her to come back before he could add more wives (1 Sam. 27:3).

Likewise, if Marsha were to divorce her husband, Bill, for irreconcilable differences and marry Rick, Bill could marry Suzy and wouldn't commit adultery. What's imperative to know is that God doesn't recognize divorce, so Bill would, in fact, have two wives; and if Marsha should reconcile, he must take her back. If Bill were to rebuff Marsha's reconciliation attempts, he would be guilty of adultery. Nowhere in scripture will one find a passage that is a male version of Romans 7; this is because, as we have already seen, polygyny is lawful for men.

One important caveat is that God will judge all of us by our actions and intentions, so if a man were to treat his wife terribly to drive her to divorce him so he could marry another woman, God would look at him no differently than if he'd divorced her. This is no different, then, when someone doesn't return a lost item when he or she knows who the rightful owner is (Deut. 22:1–4).

In keeping with the legitimacy of polygyny, it's impossible for a single woman to commit adultery. Scripture condemns a man for having sex with another man's wife or a divorced woman, but it doesn't condemn a man who doesn't initiate a divorce against his wife and marries another. Consider a single woman who is living with a divorced man; even though she isn't sinning, she effectively prevents him from ever reconciling with God. A man who divorces his wife must remain a eunuch for the kingdom of heaven or reconcile with his wife. If a man divorces his wife and doesn't marry another woman, but instead has sex with a girlfriend or prostitute, it still qualifies as adultery, much like if a divorced woman were to have sex with a boyfriend and avoid remarriage. The reason is that he has turned his back on his wife, so God doesn't see a remarriage or any sexual relationship on his part as legitimate.

The story of John the Baptist's death is rather intriguing, and proponents of divorce and remarriage tend to shy away from it. It's rather amazing that the greatest man born of a woman (Luke 7:28) died because he spoke boldly about Herod and Herodias's adultery. Those brave enough to tackle this story state that John was preaching against an incestuous relationship rather than adultery. However, what they fail to take into account is that John was, in fact, preaching against an adulterous remarriage and an incestuous relationship; it doesn't have to be one or the other. But if one were forced to choose, it would seem rather obvious, when reading scripture, that John condemned adultery. Mark 6:17–20 says,

> For Herod himself had sent forth and laid hold upon John, and bound him in prison for Herodias' sake, his brother Philip's wife: for he had married her. For John had said unto Herod, It is not lawful for thee to have thy brother's wife. Therefore Herodias had a quarrel against him, and would have killed him; but she could not: For Herod feared John, knowing that he was a just man and an holy, and observed him; and when he heard him, he did many things, and heard him gladly.

We can glean several facts that further refute divorce and remarriage. Herodias's adultery with Herod didn't end her marriage with Philip, nor did her abandonment of Philip. Despite the fact that Herodias went through the proper legal route according to Roman law, this didn't make the remarriage legal in God's eyes. An interesting factoid people don't often mention is that while John rebuked Herod and Herodias's adulterous relationship, he said absolutely nothing about Herod's other wives (Josephus says he had nine).[1]

In summary, a man who divorces his wife and marries another woman commits adultery, and any man who marries a divorced woman commits adultery. There is no exception clause in scripture, and even if we do assume that there is one, it doesn't make any logical sense. No one can find any verse in the Bible that permits someone to divorce his or her spouse and remarry. To repent, one must forsake his or her sin, not continue in it.

The author acknowledges that situations can get quite convoluted in cases where Bill married Marsha, but she was previously married to Tim, who in turn was married to Jill. Did Tim divorce Jill to marry Marsha? Was Tim innocent and Jill just decided to leave him? Was Jill herself previously married? If Bill doesn't know all the details in such circumstances, he would have to be a eunuch for the kingdom of heaven's sake. We know adulterers won't make it into heaven, but no one who abstains from sex will be barred entry. In such a case where Bill married Marsha, who divorced Tim, and it was both Marsha and Tim's first marriage, Bill would be free to marry because his relationship with Marsha was adulterous. This is because he knew for certain that Marsha was still married to Tim.

God isn't to blame for this confusion; if men preached and taught his Word like they should, this wouldn't be a problem. When God says, "Don't do x" and man says "You can do x under certain circumstances," we will always have problems. Hopefully this will be the start of a movement to return to and obey God's laws in respect to marriage.

Marriage isn't some contract or business arrangement that can be modified or dissolved by simply going to court. It doesn't need to be, nor is it, defined by government, but by God. God doesn't need a judge or even a pastor to make it official. All he needs is just a commitment between one man and at least one woman who agree to live as one and are united until death.

CHAPTER 4

Sex Outside of Wedlock and Rape

WE NOW TURN TO UNMARRIED sex outside of wedlock, which is permitted under God's law—except rape, which is condemned. God regulated prostitution, which in turn proves its legality. Deuteronomy 23:17–18 says,

> There shall be no whore of the daughters of Israel, nor a sodomite of the sons of Israel. Thou shalt not bring the hire of a whore, or the price of a dog, into the house of the Lord thy God for any vow: for even both these are abomination unto the Lord thy God.

Deuteronomy 23:17–18 refers to a female temple prostitute (*q'deshah*) and a male temple prostitute (*qadesh*), respectively. In verse 18 God forbade anyone from bringing in the hire of a whore (*zanah*) or the price of a dog (*keleb*) into his temple because it was an abomination to him. The context shows that the whore and dog in verse 18 are also the temple prostitutes in verse 17. Unfortunately, the King James translation has created many problems over the years; if we take it at face value, we will create a lot of contradictions throughout the scriptures, as we will see. Fortunately, many Bible translations have begun to properly translate the verse as condemning cult, temple, or sacred prostitution due to the Hebrew words *qadesh* and *qedeshah*, which refer to males and females, respectively, and mean "sacred" or "holy." This is important to note because there are times in scripture when the word *zanah* is used to refer to temple prostitutes or people having sex as a form of worship to a god. The context is important to understand when looking at the word *zanah* and *porneia* in scripture.

Depending on the context, this could refer to temple prostitution or sexual idolatry, and the word *zanah* could be used instead of *qadesh* or *q'deshah*. Some Christians rightly state that premarital sex isn't a sin; however, they incorrectly say that *zanah* and *porneia* don't include premarital sex. In fact, they do, as we shall see. Premarital sex will be defined in this book as consensual sex that doesn't violate any of God's laws regarding sex. It should be clear by now, having dealt with lust and adultery, that an unmarried woman cannot commit adultery, regardless of the marital status of the man. So how can it be sin for an unmarried woman to sleep with a man, whether he is single or married? The fact is that it's not sin, which is why, as we will see, some men of God had sex with prostitutes without any condemnation from God.

Another regulation God established in regard to prostitution was that he forbade fathers from pimping their daughters through forced prostitution. Leviticus 19:29 says, "Do not prostitute thy daughter, to cause her to be a whore; lest the land fall to whoredom, and the land become full of wickedness." If a woman wasn't under her father's care, this law didn't apply. If a father forced his daughter into prostitution, it would be a sin, though no blood sacrifice was mentioned. It would violate the fruit of the Spirit.

Leviticus 21:9 says, "And the daughter of any priest, if she profane herself by playing the whore, she profaneth her father: she shall be burnt with fire." This law is related to sexual idolatry just like Deuteronomy 23:17–18; this regulation prevented men from having sex with a priest's daughter as a form of worship to God. God didn't want to have anything whatsoever to do with sexual idolatry, so the Levi priests' daughters couldn't have sex outside of marriage. These were the only laws specifically regulating prostitution in Israel. Note that one doesn't have to have sex with a temple prostitute to commit sexual idolatry. All that is required is to have sex in honor of, or worship to, an idol; during Old Testament times, a sacrifice usually accompanied this.

One such example is when the Israelites were in the wilderness, and Aaron made a golden calf "and the people began to eat and drink and rose up to play" (Exod. 32:6). The Hebrew word for "play" is *taschaq*, which means to play or make sport; this denotes that sexual activity was taking place in addition to the idolatry involved with worshipping the golden calf. No temple prostitutes were present, but the event still qualifies as sexual idolatry. Also note there was sacrifice involved with the worship of the idol. Sacrifice in connection with fornication (*porneia*) and whoredom (*zanah*) is a common theme throughout the Bible.

This type of whoredom or fornication is sin, but one must pay attention to the context, since the scribes used the terms whoredom and fornication rather liberally. So many Christians unintentionally ignore the context and simply make a judgment based off the words "fornication" and "whoredom." The consequences of this poor exegesis lead to incorrect doctrine, which causes many people to stumble. Now let's analyze the story of the much-maligned Samson. Judges 15:1–2, 6, 14–15 says,

> But it came to pass within a while after, in the time of wheat harvest, that Samson visited his wife with a kid; and he said, I will go in to my wife into the chamber. But her father would not suffer him to go in. And her father said, I verily thought that thou hadst utterly hated her; therefore I gave her to thy companion: is not her younger sister fairer than she? take her, I pray thee, instead of her…Then the Philistines said, Who hath done this? And they answered, Samson, the son in law of the Timnite, because he had taken his wife, and given her to his companion. And the Philistines came up, and burnt her and her father with fire…And when he came unto Lehi, the Philistines shouted against him: and the Spirit of the Lord came mightily upon him, and the cords that were upon his arms became as flax that was burnt with fire, and his bands loosed from off his hands. And he found a new jawbone of an ass, and put forth his hand, and took it, and slew a thousand men therewith.

Although Samson shouldn't have married a Philistine, his marriage was still valid. Some question the fact that God gave Samson the supernatural strength to kill the Philistines; still, he didn't sin by marrying a Philistine any more than a Christian who marries an unbeliever. Many of the same

Christians who criticize Samson teach that a marriage between a believer and an unbeliever is valid; they can't seem to grasp their own hypocrisy. Samson is most often criticized for sleeping with a prostitute (Judg. 16:1); however, the Spirit of the Lord was still upon him and didn't depart because of this activity. If Samson's critics had actually studied the Word of God, they wouldn't foolishly be at a loss as to explain why the Spirit of the Lord didn't depart until after his hair had been cut (Judg. 16:19). If they bothered to study God's law in regard to sex, they would have known that sleeping with a prostitute was, in fact, not a sin.

Critics often insist that Samson's having sex with a prostitute was just another one of his sins for which God chose to look the other way, much like he did when Samson married a Philistine and got honey from a dead lion. We've already seen that he didn't sin by marrying a Philistine; he also didn't sin by getting honey from a dead lion.

> Speak unto the children of Israel, and say unto them, When either man or woman shall separate themselves to vow a vow of a Nazarite, to separate themselves unto the Lord: He shall separate himself from wine and strong drink, and shall drink no vinegar of wine, or vinegar of strong drink, neither shall he drink any liquor of grapes, nor eat moist grapes, or dried. All the days of his separation shall he eat nothing that is made of the vine tree, from the kernels even to the husk. All the days of the vow of his separation there shall no rasor come upon his head: until the days be fulfilled, in the which he separateth himself unto the Lord, he shall be holy, and shall let the locks of the hair of his head grow. All the days that he separateth himself unto the Lord he shall come at no dead body. He shall not make himself unclean for his father, or for his mother, for his brother, or for his sister, when they die: because the consecration of his God is upon his head. All the days of his separation he is holy unto the Lord. (Num. 6:2–8)

Many Christians have incorrectly argued for years that Samson sinned because he touched the carcass of a dead lion (Judg. 14:9). However, nothing

Sex Outside of Wedlock and Rape

in the Nazarite vow actually condemned touching a dead animal. It simply mentioned this in relation to human bodies, since it forbade burying them or attending a burial service. This prohibition on funeral services is similar to that of the high priest (Lev. 21:11), so, in fact, Samson didn't break his vow by eating honey from a lion. Does anyone really think God would put his Spirit on Samson while he broke the vow he was supposed to keep? It's famously recorded that Samson killed Philistines with the jawbone of an ass (Judg. 15:15), but at no time is it recorded that Samson killed anyone with his bare hands or touched a dead man. Keep in mind that it was God's working in Samson that gave him his supernatural strength. Would God break his own law?

Judges 16:19–21 says,

> And she made him sleep upon her knees; and she called for a man, and she caused him to shave off the seven locks of his head; and she began to afflict him, and his strength went from him. And she said, The Philistines be upon thee, Samson. And he awoke out of his sleep, and said, I will go out as at other times before, and shake myself. And he wist not that the Lord was departed from him. But the Philistines took him, and put out his eyes, and brought him down to Gaza, and bound him with fetters of brass; and he did grind in the prison house.

It wasn't until the Philistines cut off Samson's locks that the Spirit of God departed from him; this was because he'd broken the Nazarite vow. It's rather silly to believe God would look the other way when Samson had sex with a prostitute and ate honey from a dead lion but didn't tolerate his hair being cut, even when someone else did it. God's Spirit departing from him is further proof that he hadn't broken his vow by participating in any of his previous actions.

The Bible tells us that Samson slept at Delilah's knees; this is more than likely referring to postcoital sleep. Scripture also mentions his "grinding" in the prison. By comparing scripture with scripture, we can determine that this grinding was, in fact, sex—Samson had sex with women the Philistines brought to him. This same word, "grind" (*tachan*), is used by Job in Job 31:10: "Then let my wife grind unto another, and let others bow down upon her."

The Philistines, not believing in the one true God, believed they could produce strongmen from Samson's seed; they didn't realize his power came supernaturally from God. It's rather sad that so many Christians hold the "Disney" view of scripture; nowhere is it mentioned that Samson ground crops or worked the mill. There isn't even any evidence that the Philistines had such devices in their prisons.

Since Christianity has become sexually puritanical over time, proponents of "purity" insist that prostitution is a sin despite evidence to the contrary. Prostitution is prohibited only in terms of sexual idolatry, evident by the fact that God didn't depart from Samson when he slept with a prostitute. Jesus was clear that he didn't come to abolish the law (Matt. 5:17), and God himself said we shouldn't add to or diminish his law (Deut. 4:2). It's OK, then, to have sex with a prostitute provided that none of God's other laws are violated. When people try to argue that prostitution is a sin based on the New Testament, they may not be aware that they effectively try to make the Word of God contradict itself, because the New Testament is based on the Old.

Most Christians believe the modern definition of adultery and the condemnation of prostitution while purporting to uphold God's standard. The story of Jephthah, who was the son of Gilead and a prostitute (Judg. 11:1), presents another problem to the so-called purists. How could Jephthah even have been born if all prostitutes were put to death? Not even one verse in scripture supports this false assumption of prostitution being sin. These people are stuck in a quagmire. How do they explain this away? Simple. They can't, so they usually just ignore it or appeal to generic New Testament passages that condemn "fornication." Those who try to tackle this issue fall flat on their faces, showing that their personal sexual morality is above God's—even to the point of making God's Word contradict itself in the process.

In Deuteronomy 23:2, God said that "a bastard [*mamzer*] shall not enter into the congregation of the Lord even to their tenth generation." Just as people mistakenly believe that a married man having sex with an unmarried woman is adultery, they also make a similar mistake that the biblical definition of "bastard" is a person born out of wedlock.

> Then the Spirit of the Lord came upon Jephthah, and he passed over Gilead, and Manasseh, and passed over Mizpeh of Gilead, and from Mizpeh of Gilead he passed over unto the children of Ammon. (Judg. 11:29)

> And Jephthah judged Israel six years. Then died Jephthah the Gileadite, and was buried in one of the cities of Gilead. (Judg. 12:7)

If we take the contemporary definition of "bastard" and apply it to *mamzer*, God was being hypocritical, because God's Spirit fell on Jephthah, even though he shouldn't have even been in God's congregation. To top it all off, Jephthah became a judge over Israel for six years. Even if one were to argue that this was a dark period in Israel's history, how do critics explain the fact that the Spirit of God fell on him? By evaluating scripture with scripture, we can determine that Jephthah wasn't a bastard, and this is further proof that prostitution wasn't a sin. So the Spirit of the Lord fell on him, and he led Israel as a judge without contradicting any of God's laws.

Who, then, is a *mamzer*? The truth is that we don't really know for sure. It could be someone born of an adulterous relationship when there were only one or no witnesses present to put the guilty to death. It could also be people born of an incestuous relationship who weren't put to death. The author leans toward a *mamzer* being the offspring of an Israelite parent and an unconverted parent, based on Nehemiah 13 and Ezra 9, which we discussed in detail in the previous chapter. What is important and what we do know is that Jephthah wasn't a *mamzer* despite the fact that he was born out of wedlock to a prostitute. Gilead didn't engage in any sin by having sex with a prostitute, even if his wife (wives?) was still alive.

Another account that proves prostitution isn't a sin is the famous story of Solomon offering to split the baby in two; both of the women involved were prostitutes (1 Kings 3:16–28). Solomon, in all his wisdom, never said they should be stoned for their "sin," another fact opponents like to ignore. Biblically speaking, extramarital sex is only a sin when it violates one of God's existing laws, so a married man who has sex with a single woman doesn't commit sin. A husband is under no obligation to tell his wife or wives if he even engaged in extramarital sex.

Some Old Testament passages are used from time to time to condemn prostitution, but on closer examination, they don't do this. First Samuel 2:22 says, "Now Eli was very old, and heard all that his sons did unto all Israel; and how they lay with the women that assembled at the door of the tabernacle of the congregation." The fact is that Eli's sons, Hophni and Phineas, had sex with temple prostitutes. This activity angered God, and he eventually killed both of Eli's sons (1 Sam. 2:34) for their sins. Even though the Hebrew word for "temple prostitute" isn't used here, neither is the Hebrew word for "prostitute"; but the context speaks of Eli's sons having sex with women assembled at the congregation, which would make this sexual idolatry.

We now turn to the story of Rahab, the harlot, whom the newer, politically correct versions of the Bible call an "innkeeper" or "hostess." Yet, the word used here is *zanah* in Hebrew, and the Septuagint uses the Greek word *porne*, which is the feminine version of prostitute. This is more evidence that the puritanical proponents rely on their own sexual standard and not God's.

Joshua 2:1 says, "And Joshua the son of Nun sent out of Shittim two men to spy secretly, saying, Go view the land, even Jericho. And they went, and came into an harlot's house, named Rahab, and lodged there." In addition to the fact that some try to say Rahab wasn't a harlot when scripture plainly says so, the word "lodged" is translated from *shakab*, which is also a euphemism for sex. The two spies "laid" in the house of Rahab, the prostitute (Josh. 2:1); the obvious sexual connotations can't be ignored. Would they really be spies if they went to a brothel and didn't have sex?

The G-rated version of Christianity would have the spies going to Rahab's brothel for a good night's sleep without sex and without drawing any attention whatsoever. Yet, these same people stress that *shakab* has sexual connotations in Exodus 22:16, when a man "lays" with an unpledged woman or when Leviticus 18:22 states, "Thou shalt not lie [*shakab*] with mankind as with womankind." The context is clear in all these examples that *shakab* means sex. It should be equally clear that when men go to *shakab* in a brothel, they would also be engaging in sex; not doing so would make them stand out.

Not only was God a polygynist (a sororal one at that), as we have seen in a previous chapter, but many don't know he also used the services of a prostitute. Isaiah 23:17–18 says,

> And it shall come to pass after the end of seventy years, that the Lord will visit Tyre, and she shall turn to her hire, and shall commit fornication with all the kingdoms of the world upon the face of the earth. And her merchandise and her hire shall be holiness to the Lord: it shall not be treasured nor laid up; for her merchandise shall be for them that dwell before the Lord, to eat sufficiently, and for durable clothing.

The Douay-Rheims Bible states that God visited the whore Tyre and returned her to her traffic. The puritanical proponents of sexuality don't have a leg to stand on—none of them even attempt to address this passage.

In Hosea 1:2, God told the prophet Hosea to marry a woman of whoredom (*zanuwn*) and children of whoredom (*zanuwn*); this more than likely refers to a woman who would become adulterous after marriage because this is symbolic of Israel's going after other gods. Even if one were to accept that God told Hosea to marry a prostitute, this doesn't condemn prostitution in any way because as soon as Gomer married Hosea and went after other men, adultery is the sin, not prostitution. If Gomer hadn't married Hosea, then no sin would have been committed.

The sexual "purity" crowd uses Proverbs 7:22 to condemn prostitution, but once the peephole is removed and everything is read in context, we find no verse that states prostitution is a sin:

> For at the window of my house I looked through my casement, And beheld among the simple ones, I discerned among the youths, a young man void of understanding, Passing through the street near her corner; and he went the way to her house, In the twilight, in the evening, in the black and dark night: And, behold, there met him a woman with the attire of an harlot, and subtil of heart. (She is loud and stubborn; her feet abide not in her house: Now is she without, now in the streets, and lieth in wait at every corner.) So she caught him, and kissed him, and with an impudent face said unto him, I have peace offerings with me; this day have I payed my vows. Therefore came I forth to meet thee, diligently to seek thy face, and I have found thee. I have decked my bed with coverings of tapestry, with carved works, with fine linen of Egypt. I have perfumed my bed with myrrh, aloes, and cinnamon. Come, let us take our fill of love until the morning: let us solace ourselves with loves. For the goodman is not at home, he is gone a long journey: He hath taken a bag of money with him, and will come home at the day appointed. With her much fair speech she caused him to yield, with the flattering of her lips she forced him. He goeth after her straightway, as an ox goeth to the slaughter, or as a fool to the correction of the stocks; Till a dart strike through his liver; as a bird hasteth to the snare, and knoweth not that it is for his life. (Prov. 7:6–23)

Based on their context, these verses have nothing to do with prostitution. Scripture says that she has an attire of a prostitute; she only appears like one to have sex. In reality, she is a married woman whose husband is away from home. This is why it says she abides not in her house—because she is out on the streets, looking for a man, dressed like a prostitute to ensnare him. The word "goodman" is translated from the Hebrew word *iysh*, which can mean "man" or "husband"; the context dictates that this should be "husband," because she is looking for sex while he is away and will be coming back to his home. A man who uses the services of a prostitute doesn't live with her; he has his own house to go to, and if there was another man with a prostitute, he wouldn't be surprised because other men use the services of a prostitute.

Why would he care if she has sex with another man when he isn't using her services? However, if this is her husband, it makes perfect sense. Also notice that sex with her will cost the young man his life; we know that the sin of adultery carried the death penalty and that God issued no such punishment for common prostitution because it was lawful, so this could be referring only to an adulterous woman. The sexual crusaders having nothing to back up their beliefs, so they use tactics like saying the previous passage in Proverbs condemns prostitution and sex outside of wedlock in general, when it condemns adultery. They mostly rely on taking bits and pieces of scripture and hoping their audience doesn't catch on.

> My people ask counsel at their stocks, and their staff declareth unto them: for the spirit of whoredoms hath caused them to err, and they have gone a whoring from under their God. They sacrifice upon the tops of the mountains, and burn incense upon the hills, under oaks and poplars and elms, because the shadow thereof is good: therefore your daughters shall commit whoredom, and your spouses shall commit adultery. I will not punish your daughters when they commit whoredom, nor your spouses when they commit adultery: for themselves are separated with whores, and they sacrifice with harlots: therefore the people that doth not understand shall fall. Though thou, Israel, play the harlot, yet let not Judah offend; and come not ye unto Gilgal, neither go ye up to Bethaven, nor swear, The Lord liveth. For Israel slideth back as a backsliding heifer: now the Lord will feed them as a lamb in a large place. Ephraim is joined to idols: let him alone. Their drink is sour: they have committed whoredom continually: her rulers with shame do love, Give ye. The wind hath bound her up in her wings, and they shall be ashamed because of their sacrifices. (Hos. 4:12–19)

When the sexual crusaders cite this passage, they usually focus on verses 12–14 in isolation and ignore the context of scripture. However, when we read the verses in context, it is evident that the Israelites were committing sexual idolatry and sacrificing to other gods. Some were committing this sin with temple prostitutes; some were doing this with other men's wives—hence adultery. Still others were doing it with other unmarried women of Israel, which is why their daughters committed whoredom. This is why God said he wouldn't punish their wives or daughters; the men were committing the same sin they were. Verse 15 calls or portrays Israel as a harlot because the people had gone worshipping strange gods through sex with temple prostitutes, other men's wives, and/or women in general. One fact they all had in common was that they were sacrificing to these gods and burning incense to them.

Of all Jesus's sayings, probably the least quoted one involves prostitution. Not surprisingly, modern-day sexual crusaders don't know how to handle this quote. Most simply ignore it, while others shrug it off and say it is spurious (which is an easy cop-out). But the ones bold enough to respond to Jesus's quote will say that only former prostitutes will enter the kingdom of heaven. Matthew 21:31–32 says,

> Jesus saith unto them, Verily I say unto you, That the publicans and the harlots go into the kingdom of God before you. For John came unto you in the way of righteousness, and ye believed him not: but the publicans and the harlots believed him: and ye, when ye had seen it, repented not afterward, that ye might believe him.

The only problem is that Jesus never said "former" prostitutes or publicans enter the kingdom of heaven ahead of the Pharisees. Indeed, both the publicans and prostitutes continue to practice their profession and enter (the Greek uses the present tense) the kingdom ahead of them. Both Jesus and John the Baptist knew God's law, and Jesus stated that John had disciples who were prostitutes and publicans. We also know Jesus had disciples who were publicans; as long as they weren't robbing people, they could continue to hold their profession. So it isn't a stretch to say that some, or maybe even most, of the women who followed Jesus were prostitutes.

When we consider the fact that women's career choices were extremely limited at the time, it's hard to imagine that married women who had to raise several children were following him. It's much easier to imagine that these women were prostitutes, widows with no children, or women whose children were grown. The only realistic way a married woman with children could have seen Jesus was if he came to her town; only the previously mentioned women could have followed Jesus to multiple cities. So it isn't unreasonable to conclude that Mary Magdalene was a prostitute; she was more than likely to support herself by practicing prostitution. Even if the reader rejects the theory that Mary Magdalene was a prostitute, this in no way refutes the fact that prostitution isn't a sin and that prostitutes are still entering the kingdom of heaven.

One of the most famous parts of the Bible people try to use to condemn unmarried sex is the story of the Midianites or Moabites and how they caused Israel to fall. The Moabites and Midianites feared that the Israelites would overrun them, since they defeated everyone in their path and already had an established reputation in war. The original plan was to hire Balaam to curse the Israelites; the problem was that Balaam couldn't curse what God had already blessed (Num. 24:9). Balaam, however, cast a stumbling block before Israel by having the children of Israel eat things sacrificed to idols and commit fornication (Rev. 2:14).

Numbers 25:1–3 says,

> And Israel abode in Shittim, and the people began to commit whoredom with the daughters of Moab. And they called the people unto the sacrifices of their gods: and the people did eat, and bowed down to their gods. And Israel joined himself unto Baalpeor: and the anger of the Lord was kindled against Israel.

Notice that Israel joined Baalpeor; the sacrificing to this god and having sex with the Moabite women are what caused God to be angry with the

Israelites. They were joined with another god; sexual idolatry is the sin of which they were guilty. On closer examination, we see that this incident has nothing to do with unmarried sex. Why would it be, considering what we've already discovered in regard to common prostitution? God ultimately sent a plague against Israel as punishment and killed twenty-four thousand men for the sin of sexual idolatry (Num. 25:9). It's important to keep in mind the sins Israel committed with the Moabites and Midianites. Paul alluded to them in the book of Corinthians.

The books of Joshua and Samuel mention the book of Jasher. This incident is recorded in more detail and aligns with the story found in Numbers.

> And the children of Israel approached Moab, and the children of Moab pitched their tents opposite to the camp of the children of Israel. And the children of Moab were afraid of the children of Israel, and the children of Moab took all their daughters and their wives of beautiful aspect and comely appearance, and dressed them in gold and silver and costly garments. And the children of Moab seated those women at the door of their tents, in order that the children of Israel might see them and turn to them, and not fight against Moab. And all the children of Moab did this thing to the children of Israel, and every man placed his wife and daughter at the door of his tent, and all the children of Israel saw the act of the children of Moab, and the children of Israel turned to the daughters of Moab and coveted them, and they went to them. And it came to pass that when a Hebrew came to the door of the tent of Moab, and saw a daughter of Moab and desired her in his heart, and spoke with her at the door of the tent that which he desired, whilst they were speaking together the men of the tent would come out and speak to the Hebrew like unto these words: Surely you know that we are brethren, we are all the descendants of Lot and the descendants of Abraham his brother, wherefore then will you not remain with us, and wherefore will you not eat our bread and our sacrifice? And

Sex Outside of Wedlock and Rape

> when the children of Moab had thus overwhelmed him with their speeches, and enticed him by their flattering words, they seated him in the tent and cooked and sacrificed for him, and he ate of their sacrifice and of their bread. They then gave him wine and he drank and became intoxicated, and they placed before him a beautiful damsel, and he did with her as he liked, for he knew not what he was doing, as he had drunk plentifully of wine. Thus did the children of Moab to Israel in that place, in the plain of Shittim, and the anger of the Lord was kindled against Israel on account of this matter, and he sent a pestilence amongst them, and there died of the Israelites twenty-four thousand men. (Jash. 85:53–61)

In Numbers 25:4, God told Moses to hang all the leaders of Israel for their sins. Moses then told the judges to kill all the men joined with Baalpeor (Num. 25:4–5). On top of this, God sent a plague against Israel because of their sins. In spite of what was going on there, an Israelite named Zimri brought a Midianite woman, Cozbi, in front of Moses and the congregation, and he proceeded to have sex with her while the Israelites were bemoaning their sins. This brazen act of sin led Eleazar's son Phinehas to kill the couple engaging in this heinous act with a javelin, piercing both of them in the very act (Num. 25:6). This immediately stopped the plague God had sent for Israel's sin of sexual idolatry, but not before twenty-four thousand Israelites died (Num. 25:9).

It's bad enough to worship another god; worse still is to worship another god through sex and sacrifice. But to brazenly worship another god through sex in front of the entire congregation, while they repent of their sins and while God has sent a plague, is easily one of the most arrogant acts recorded in scripture. For the act of killing Zimri, God not only ceased the plagues against Israel but also blessed Phinehas by giving him a covenant of peace and making him and his seed an age-lasting priesthood (Num. 25:11–12).

In Numbers 25:15–18, God told Moses to kill the Midianites because they had caused the Israelites to sin against him. The Israelites would send their army to destroy the Midianite kings and their males—even Balaam (Num. 31:7–8)—but there was a problem. The Israelites took all the women captive, including the children (Num. 31:11). When Moses learned that they'd kept all the Midianite women alive, he was upset (Num. 31:16). The reason for his anger was obvious; the women who had committed sexual idolatry with the Israelites were the reason for Israel's sin in the first place. So why would they keep them alive? Moses commanded them to kill all the boys and nonvirgin women and to keep the virgins for themselves (Num. 31:17–18). This made perfect sense because the penalty for idolatry was death, and all the Israelites who'd committed this act were already dead, either by the plague God had sent or through the judges, who were told to hang all the men who had sex with them (Num. 25:5). They were allowed to keep all the virgins because they weren't guilty of the sin of sexual idolatry; these female captives would fall under the law detailed in Deuteronomy 21.

> When thou goest forth to war against thine enemies, and the Lord thy God hath delivered them into thine hands, and thou hast taken them captive, And seest among the captives a beautiful woman, and hast a desire unto her, that thou wouldest have her to thy wife; Then thou shalt bring her home to thine house; and she shall shave her head, and pare her nails; And she shall put the raiment of her captivity from off her, and shall remain in thine house, and bewail her father and her mother a full month: and after that thou shalt go in unto her, and be her husband, and she shall be thy wife. And it shall be, if thou have no delight in her, then thou shalt let her go whither she will; but thou shalt not sell her at all for money, thou shalt not make merchandise of her, because thou hast humbled her. (vv. 10–14)

We must remember that the Hebrew words for "husband" and "wife" could also mean "man" and "woman"; these words in the Hebrew are used as such from time to time. This was not a marriage; that no divorce is mentioned further supports this claim: she was simply released. She couldn't be sold into slavery to someone else because she had already been held against her will when she was initially taken captive; this is why people refer to this as the "law of the captive woman." Many of the sexual crusaders admit she was a captive but state that the captor didn't have sex with her; his humbling her refutes this claim. The Hebrew word *anah*, which is translated "humbled," is also used in Deuteronomy 22:24 and describes adultery and rape in Deuteronomy 22:29. Therefore, it is rather absurd to say this doesn't mean sex in regard to the law of the captive woman.

Unfortunately, so many people incorrectly believe unmarried sex was the reason Israel stumbled; in fact, sexual idolatry was the culprit. Too many Christians view sex in the Bible anachronistically. Instead of viewing it puritanically, they should view it as it is in the Word of God. Now we've seen that the reason the Israelites fell into sin was sexual idolatry with the Midianites and the Moabites. Paul's writings in Corinthians become clear and, more importantly, consistent with the Old Testament. Remember, God himself said there was nothing to add to his Word, and we have already seen that Jesus didn't add to it either. So why would Paul?

While Paul was in Corinth, he realized that the Christians there were committing the same sin of sexual idolatry the Israelites had committed with the Midianites and Moabites. First Corinthians 6:15–19 says,

> Know ye not that your bodies are the members of Christ? shall I then take the members of Christ, and make them the members of an harlot? God forbid. What? know ye not that he which is joined to an harlot is one body? for two, saith he, shall be one flesh. But he that is joined unto the Lord is one spirit. Flee fornication. Every sin that a man doeth is without the body; but he that committeth fornication sinneth against his own body. What? know ye not that your body is the temple of the Holy Ghost which is in you, which ye have of God, and ye are not your own?

Paul made the obvious comparison of the Christians at Corinth having sex with temple prostitutes as a form of worship to pagan gods with the Israelites having sex as a form of worship to Baalpeor. Paul said that every sin a man commits is without the body except for fornication (*porneia*), which in this case refers to temple prostitutes and sexual idolatry. It can also include all other sexual sins, such as adultery, rape, incest, and so forth. As we've noticed in the Old Testament, sometimes the Hebrew word for "temple prostitute" isn't used; only the regular word for "prostitute" is used, so we must pay attention to the context. The context Paul talked about here is temple prostitutes. Even though there's no distinction made between common and sacred prostitution in the Greek manuscripts, this doesn't condemn common prostitution any more than the lack of distinction in many Hebrew passages.

By now it should be clear that common prostitution isn't a sin; only sexual idolatry is condemned. Those who insist it is condemned in the New Testament must find a way to explain this contradiction in light of God and Jesus's statement in regard to the law. Those who have an ear to hear and eyes to see know Paul condemned sexual idolatry taking place in Corinth. This is why Paul stated that when a believer, who was part of the body of Christ, had sex with a temple prostitute, he or she took the member of Christ and joined it with another god. But the believer is supposed to be one spirit to one God (1 Cor. 6:17). This is no different than when the Israelites, who were already married to God, engaged in sexual idolatry with the Midianites or Moabites and joined themselves with Baalpeor in the process.

A Christian shouldn't do such a thing because his or her body is the temple of the Lord; to say this prohibition also refers to common prostitution contradicts God's law because the Old Testament doesn't condemn such behavior. So God would contradict himself by saying it wasn't a sin then but is a sin now. Why would Paul say common prostitution is a sin when the Spirit of the Lord was upon Samson, even when he was having sex with a prostitute? God doesn't have a problem with common prostitution any more than he does with any other profession, such as plumbing; what he does have a problem with is lying, stealing, killing, and so forth.

In 1 Corinthians 10:7, Paul saw the parallels with the Christians in Corinth and the Israelites, who were idolaters and rose up to play, eat, and drink. We've already seen that this festival included sex in honor of the golden calf in Exodus 32:6. Paul also told Christians in Corinth not to commit fornication like the Israelites did, which resulted in twenty-three thousand dead (1 Cor. 10:8). Even though there is a discrepancy in the number of people killed, the reference still obviously alludes to God's punishment mentioned in Numbers 25:9.

The sexual crusaders' favorite proof text in Corinthians, used to "prove" that unmarried sex is sin, falls apart. There can be no doubt that Paul referenced the twenty-four thousand God killed by plague because of the sin of sexual idolatry. Worshipping Baalpeor by having sex with the Midianites and Moabites and sacrificing to their gods will incur the wrath of God every time. There's no need to argue about what ancient Greek historian Strabo said or didn't say about the temple of Aphrodite in Corinth; it is irrelevant to argue one way or the other. By comparing scripture with scripture, we know sexual idolatry is the sin that was committed. Since we know Paul didn't condemn common prostitution, we also know sex outside of wedlock isn't sin either.

Another verse that critics might appeal to is Joel 3:3, which talks about giving a boy for a harlot. This isn't a condemnation of prostitution in general but only of the method of transaction. You cannot condemn alcohol just because a girl was sold for a bottle of wine; only the transaction is at fault here. One of the opponents' favorite verses is Leviticus 21:9, which states that the daughter of any priest who plays the whore must be burned with fire. But as we have already seen, this verse is related to sexual idolatry because the law was only for the tribe of Levi, which comprised God's priests. If you were from any other tribe, a foreigner, or even a Levite and not a priest, this law didn't apply.

The argument at this point might shift to 1 Peter 2:9, which states that all Christians are priests; therefore, you cannot be a Christian and a prostitute. But this reasoning has numerous problems. First of all, this law didn't forbid priests from having sex with a prostitute. A Levitical priest could have sex with a prostitute provided she wasn't a temple prostitute. So this law cannot condemn Christians from using the services of a prostitute. More importantly, scripture states we are all priests, but this analogy goes only so far. Christians are also referred to as slaves, children, and brides. Yet all these analogies can go only so far logically. One cannot cherry-pick this verse; if we're all priests but cannot engage in any sex out of wedlock, then one must also come to the conclusion that all the following were forbidden from being priests:

1. The blind
2. Someone who was broken footed or broken handed
3. A humpback
4. A dwarf
5. Anyone with an itching disease
6. A eunuch
7. Anyone with a blemish not previously named

All these people were forbidden from being priests (Lev. 21:18–21), so if the all-believers-are-priests analogy is taken to its logical conclusion, the previously mentioned people couldn't have been priests. One must not forget that priests could marry only virgins (Lev. 21:13), and only the virginity of the woman is mentioned. No Christian in his or her right mind would say that being a humpback or a Christian woman who wasn't a virgin at the time of her marriage isn't valid, so you cannot logically say that prostitutes can't be Christians and ignore these other laws. Either they all apply, or they don't. The scriptures speak of all believers being priests only in terms of being intercessors; we stand between the living, God and Jesus, and the dead, who are unbelievers. Unfortunately, too many Christians take the priest analogy too far and make Peter's statement say things he didn't intend to say.

TAMAR AND JUDAH

Now we will examine the story of Tamar, which many people have used to condemn sex out of wedlock; indeed, many use Tamar as their "ace in the hole." Genesis 38:6–30 tells the complete story. Judah took Tamar as a wife for his firstborn son, Er, but God killed him because of his wickedness. Judah told his son Onan to marry Tamar (v. 8); we should note that the Hebrew word *yabam*, translated "marry," doesn't mean marriage in the traditional sense of the word. It refers to a brother performing the duty of raising up a seed in his dead brother's name. This same word *yabam* is found in Deuteronomy 25:5, 7, which describes the Levitical vow. So even before God gave the law at Mount Sinai, this tradition wasn't a requirement (Deut. 25:5–10) but was being followed.

Onan's job wasn't to marry his sister-in-law in the true sense of the word but to have sex with her so she could bear a son, which would be her modern-day equivalent of social security. Onan was selfish and knew any resulting offspring wouldn't be his. We also get more proof that Tamar wasn't married to Onan in the traditional sense, since it says that "he went in unto his brother's wife." "His brother's wife" is translated from *ach*, meaning "kindred." Eventually God had enough of this and killed Onan.

Judah told Tamar to wait until his son, Shelah, was of age to raise up seed for her. So Tamar waited. The Bible tells us that Judah's wife died and that Shelah was of age, but he hadn't performed his duty for Tamar. Tamar wasn't getting any younger and decided to take matters into her own hands. She removed her clothes of widowhood, put on a veil, and dressed like a prostitute.

Judah was on the way to Timnath to sheer his sheep and saw her, but he didn't realize who she was. Thinking she was a prostitute, he asked what her price was for sex. Tamar asked for a goat, but in the meantime she got his signet, bracelets, and staff. When Judah's friend arrived with his payment, she was nowhere to be found; three months later Tamar was visibly pregnant. Judah commanded that she be burned with fire for committing whoredom. Tamar was brought forth to be executed, but when she returned Judah's signet and staff to identify him as the father, he had to confess her righteousness.

There is plenty of unmarried sex in this story, but what's important is that Judah was going to have Tamar executed because he'd pledged his son, Shelah, to her for marriage. So when Tamar was found to be with child, her act was obviously viewed as adultery, a foreshadowing of the law described in Deuteronomy 22:23. Judah was a hypocrite and had to confess that Tamar was more righteous than he. He had no intention of giving his son to her for marriage, despite the fact that he was going to execute her for adultery to a marriage that was never going to occur. We also know Judah wasn't that smart, given that he gave what he thought was a prostitute his signet and staff, the equivalent of a driver's license and birth certificate. Tamar, despite what so many Christians believe, wasn't a prostitute; she'd only dressed like one to entice Judah to do the duty his son wouldn't do and what he wouldn't let Shelah do.

Ironically, Judah more than likely thought Tamar was the reason for his son's death, which was why he wouldn't give Shelah to her when he came of age. Judah would end up doing the deed himself, proving to him that she wasn't the reason for his sons' deaths. Tamar was after his signet and staff so Judah would be identified as the father, because she would be pregnant outside of her "marriage" to Shelah. If Judah hadn't pledged his son to Tamar and she got pregnant by anyone else, she wouldn't have been executed for whoredom, since she would have been an unpledged widow. She would have been free to do what she wanted. The other argument people use is that Judah and Tamar sinned because this scenario was a man having sex with his daughter-in-law, but this was before the law was given. To say Judah and Tamar were guilty of incest would be no different than condemning Abraham for marrying his half sister, Sarah.

The scripture also says Jacob "knew her again no more"; there was no longer a need for Shelah to raise up seed because his father had already done so. God gave Tamar twins, who acted as two witnesses against Judah's hypocrisy. Pharez, an ancestor of Jesus, was born out of wedlock, but as we have already seen, this didn't make him a *mamzer*, since this had nothing to do with being born out of wedlock. Judah had sex with Tamar out of wedlock, but there is no condemnation of his actions anywhere in scriptures.

We now study the laws regarding sex that governed Israel in more detail. Exodus 22:16–17 says, "And if a man entice a maid that isn't betrothed, and lie with her, he shall surely endow her to be his wife. If her father utterly refuse to give her unto him, he shall pay money according to the dowry of virgins." It's important that we take the context into

Sex Outside of Wedlock and Rape

consideration. Exodus 22 begins by discussing the solution to a man's stealing, killing, or selling another man's livestock, which is for the thief to pay restitution. Exodus 22 also discusses other types of scenarios leading up to verse 16, and these all have one thing in common: they are all related to some type of financial loss. Verses 16–17 are no different. When a man married a virgin, the father was entitled to the dowry. Verses 16–17 deal with the scenario in which an unpledged woman had sex with a man. The father was still entitled to the dowry of virgins, and the couple had to get married if the father chose, or he could refuse, in which case he was still entitled to the virgin's dowry. If the man couldn't afford it, he would have to work for the father to pay it off. In the other scenarios leading up to verse 16, a man would have to pay double, but in this case he didn't have to do so; he paid the same flat rate for her dowry.

Many times people point to the "fact" that sex outside of wedlock is a sin because the man had to marry her and pay the father her dowry. The facts are that the father had a right to refuse this "penalty." Second, even if the father allowed them to marry, marriage wasn't the penalty for sin—the shedding of blood was. How can you say that a couple who had sex and were forced to marry were paying the penalty for their "sin"? Marriage doesn't atone for sin, hasn't atoned for sin, and will never atone for any sin; this is an absurd claim. Another argument sexual crusaders make is that the payment of the virgin's dowry to the father was proof that he'd sinned. This is also an absurd claim because a man paid the same virgin's dowry regardless of whether he had sex with her out of, or in, wedlock.

No one would argue that the man sinned; when he paid the dowry, he got married and had sex with her. So why do people argue that a man who paid the same dowry because he had sex with her out of wedlock was sinning? The penalty for sin wasn't paying a virgin's dowry; one had to be paid regardless of whether one married her. No shedding of blood is mentioned because no sinning took place.

People who use these verses also ignore the fact that this law was rather limited in its scope. This law applied only to virgin women who were under their father's care. As we've already seen, prostitution was legal in Israel, and prostitutes obviously weren't virgins; this law didn't apply to widows or any nonvirgin women. It didn't apply to men who were or weren't virgins because only female virgins had to be given a virgin's dowry for their father.

It's quite comical that many Christians use this example to condemn sex outside of marriage; if most of these people's daughters had sex with a high-school classmate, the vast majority probably wouldn't have wanted them to marry their classmate. When one mentions the fact that many cultures today don't even have dowries to pay for virgins, the argument becomes moot. Even if she had been a virgin and lived on her own, this law wouldn't have applied because she was no longer under the care of her father—yet another convenient oversight. This law didn't apply to women who were virgins and lived under their own care, whether they were orphans or foreigners.

Ruth and Boaz

In the book of Ruth, we read that Ruth acted rather aggressively to snag Boaz as her husband. Naomi had a relative on her husband's side who turned out to be Boaz. Ruth told her mother-in-law, Naomi, that she should go to his field and glean the ears of corn, which she was entitled to due to her economic situation. Ruth said she wanted to do this so she could find favor in his sight, but instead of just gleaning the corners, she actually asked to glean after the reapers among the sheaves, giving her access to his whole field.

This bold move worked. Boaz noticed Ruth gleaning the field and inquired about her status, at which time he was informed that she was a widow. Boaz told her she didn't have to go to another field to glean, since she could continue to glean his field. Boaz also told Ruth she could abide with his maidens and drink what his servant had drawn (Ruth 2:9). Knowing she had successfully gotten Boaz's attention and found favor in his eyes, Ruth bowed in gratitude to him; she compared herself to one of Boaz's handmaidens, even though she wasn't one of his servants (v. 13).

Naomi now offered Ruth advice on how to entice him. Her plan of seduction was for Ruth to anoint herself with oil, put on some nice clothes,

Sex Outside of Wedlock and Rape

and not make herself known. After he had eaten, drunk, and fallen asleep, she was to go to his room, uncover his feet, lie down next to him, and wait for him to tell her what to do.

The word "feet" in Hebrew is sometimes used as a euphemism for genitalia. A baby "cometh out between her feet" (Deut. 28:57), and urination is referred to as "the water of their feet" (2 Kings 18:27). The Lord said he would shave the hair off Israel's feet (Isa. 7:20), and in David's attempt to cover up his adultery, he told Uriah to go home and wash his feet (2 Sam. 11:2).

When Naomi told Ruth to uncover his "feet" and lie down beside him, she wasn't talking about taking off his sandals, as if he would sleep with them on in the first place. This was around the end of the harvest season, which would have involved a celebration; this explains why Naomi told Ruth to uncover his feet only after he had eaten and drunk. Boaz ate and drank until he was content just as Naomi said he would. He slept at the end of a heap of corn. Ruth did as she was instructed; she came in at night, uncovered his "feet," and lay down beside him. Boaz awoke and was startled that she was lying by his "feet" (Ruth 3:8). Ruth responded by telling Boaz to "spread therefore thy skirt, over thine handmaid for thou art a near kinsman" (Ruth 3:9). Ruth didn't even wait for Boaz to act; she deviated from Naomi's advice and asked him to marry her. To spread one's skirt over someone was a euphemism for marriage; God used this phrase in his relationship with Israel (Ezek. 16:8).

Unfortunately, we have to deal with the G-rated version of Christianity, which suggests that Ruth lay by Boaz's literal feet like a Labrador retriever. Besides, Boaz wasn't sleeping in a bed but at the end of a heap of corn. The fact is, Boaz was naked from the waist down. Another point to consider is the fact that Ruth wanted him to spread his cloak over her; this meant she was likely undressed, since the gesture would have made little sense if she was clothed. Boaz informed Ruth that there was another man, a near kin, who had the right of refusal; but if the nearer kinsman wouldn't marry her, he would (Ruth 3:12–13). Ruth lay down at his "feet" until morning, and Boaz said, "Let it not be known that a woman came into the floor"

(v. 13). The fact that he didn't want anyone to know Ruth had spent the night with him on the threshing floor was proof that Naomi's plan had worked. Seeing Ruth naked and realizing he himself was naked, at least from the waist down, he assumed he'd had sex with her, which explains why he wanted her to leave secretly (v. 14). When Ruth asked for marriage, he was willing to accept her, provided that the other near kinsman refused.

The nearer kinsman declined to marry her, so Boaz married Ruth to raise up seed for the deceased Mahlon so his name wouldn't be cut off (Ruth 4:10). Ruth 4:11–12 says,

> And all the people that were in the gate, and the elders, said, We are witnesses. The Lord make the woman that is come into thine house like Rachel and like Leah, which two did build the house of Israel: and do thou worthily in Ephratah, and be famous in Bethlehem: And let thy house be like the house of Pharez, whom Tamar bare unto Judah, of the seed which the Lord shall give thee of this young woman.

In conclusion, we can learn from the story of Ruth that Israelites didn't hold to the same sexual standards many Christians have today. These different standards aren't important. What is important is that at no time did Boaz or Ruth commit any sin. That's right—not one sin was committed. Unfortunately, Christians hold fast to their own standards and disregard God's. The result is embarrassingly silly conclusions, such as saying that Ruth literally slept at Boaz's feet that night. They either really believe Ruth dolled herself up that night to do such a thing, or they know "feet" is being used as a euphemism, and they purposefully overlook the matter altogether.

Too many Christians fail to teach the true story of Ruth and that her aggressiveness was a good thing. Sometimes a woman has to take matters into her own hands, as both Tamar and Ruth demonstrated. Shelah was already of age, yet Judah didn't allow him to do his brother's duty; if Tamar had continued to sit idly by, she would have eventually been past childbearing age. Ruth could have just played it safe and gleaned from the corners of Boaz's field like the rest of the poor. More than likely, she would have stayed poor and single for the rest of her life.

But she had help from her mother-in-law on how to seduce Boaz, and she even took things a bit further to marry him. Most Christian women aren't taught or are aware of these things and sit idly by and just wait. Boaz didn't have to marry Ruth because the Levitical vow wasn't a requirement; if it had been, the nearer kinsman wouldn't have had the option to decline marrying Ruth. We cannot say for sure whether they had sex on the threshing floor, but we do know that at the very least, Ruth uncovered his genitals and slept with him over the night. Liken this to a woman sneaking up to a man who fell asleep after a party, taking his pants and underwear off, and lying next to him until the morning. Many Christians would consider such a woman to be a slut, but Ruth was righteous. In this age the institutional church looks for various gimmicks to attract a large crowd, such as putting a bed in the church and talking about sex in an attempt to be relevant in the eyes of the world. These church leaders altogether ignore the text or use ridiculous hermeneutics to say Ruth lay at Boaz's literal feet. Such corny nonsense deserves to be mocked. How can Christianity be taken seriously with this type of thinking?

ESTHER

In the story of Esther, many Christians purposefully ignore the details about the events that led to her becoming queen. King Ahasuerus, who ruled Persia, made a feast that included the princes, noblemen, and other dignitaries in his kingdom. The king asked his wife, Queen Vashti, to come out and parade herself in front of his guests, but she refused to come out. We aren't told why Queen Vashti chose not to come out to the king's guests; most Christians believe she was to be paraded naked before the king's guests, wearing only her crown. But nowhere does scripture say this. This type of eisegesis is all too common among Christians and leads to many errors that over time become accepted as fact. Keep in mind here that King Ahasuerus had festivities going on for over half a year; he showed the riches and majesty of his kingdom, and he wanted to show off his wife.

He didn't ask her to come out naked but to wear her crown, which would have been the ultimate way for any king to show off his wife. For whatever reason Christians have a hard time acknowledging the fact that the king would want to parade his wife around in front of his guests; he wanted to show all his possessions, since he was doing this during the high point of his festivities.

Scripture teaches that a wife is also a husband's possession, which was why he wanted her to wear her crown; to show her off in front of his guests is what most men would want to do. Why would a king who held a party not want his wife to at least make a brief appearance? For all we know, she could have been dressed conservatively. Instead of making numerous excuses for her, as so many Christians do, we might say she could have refused to show up because she simply didn't want to. The author's guess is as good as anyone else's. So how could anyone even say she was courageous and honorable?

Since the queen was disobedient to her husband, the king decided to talk to his advisers and decide what to do with her. This was a pretty rational response from the king who many claim was drunk (scripture says he was content, not drunk). The Hebrew word *towb* is used to describe the king's mood; it means "good, content, and cheerful"; it is similar to *yata*, which described Boaz's drinking (Ruth 3:7), which is defined by the same adjectives. If the scribes had wanted to let us know King Ahasuerus was drunk, they would have told us he was unaware of what was going on, similar to Lot (Gen. 19:30–38), or they would have used the Hebrew adjective *shaker* to describe him as the scribes did Noah (Gen. 9:21).

His advisers told him Queen Vashti was not only wrong in disobeying the king but also might set a bad example for other women throughout his kingdom to disobey their husbands. One of his advisers, Memucan, told the king to have her relieved of her royal title and duties, and she never presented herself in the king's presence again. This was pretty sober advice

Sex Outside of Wedlock and Rape

coming from a man who was also supposedly drunk; King Ahasuerus set about issuing a decree, whereby officers gathered fair, young virgins together so the king could choose one to be the new queen.

Esther, whom her uncle Mordecai had raised, was one of the women to make it into the king's harem after one of the officers selected her. We are told that the king's final stage for selecting a queen included twelve months of purification and a night spent with the king, culminating with sex. Ultimately, the king would choose the best woman to be queen; the women who didn't get selected would stay in the king's harem (Esther 2:14) and become a concubine. After each woman spent the night with the king, she went directly to the custody of Shaashgaz, the keeper of the concubines. She stayed there unless the king requested to see her.

Esther spent a night with the king as countless other women did, but she became the king's favorite and queen of the Persian Empire. In spite of what corny Christian movies may say, in reality a better title than "One Night with the King" would be "One-Night Stand with the King." The king was so ecstatic with the contest that he would do another round (Esther 2:19).

Some argue that Esther sinned by marrying a foreign king, but as was stated earlier in chapter 3, being unequally yoked with an unbeliever is against God's law but isn't a sin (1 Cor. 7:12–13). Nor does it nullify the marriage, as Paul affirmed in the New Testament when he commanded believers not to abandon their unbelieving spouses. Esther isn't recorded as breaking any of God's laws in regard to sex, and most Christians don't notice this important fact. Unlike Ruth, where silly arguments can be made that she literally slept at Boaz's feet, Esther is much more explicit. She had sex with the king before she became his wife. For this reason the sexual crusaders attack Esther for engaging in unmarried sex at one extreme, and at the other they attack her for being an obedient wife in contrast to Vashti (Esther 7:3–5). Thus, Esther has fallen out of favor in Western Christianity, and interestingly enough most uphold Vashti as a shining example, exposing the carnal mind-set of many modern Christians.

Concubinage

We now discuss the oft-confused practice of concubinage, which God's law regulated. Exodus 21:7–11 says,

> And if a man sell his daughter to be a maidservant, she shall not go out as the menservants do. If she please not her master, who hath betrothed her to himself, then shall he let her be redeemed: to sell her unto a strange nation he shall have no power, seeing he hath dealt deceitfully with her. And if he have betrothed her unto his son, he shall deal with her after the manner of daughters. If he take him another wife; her food, her raiment, and her duty of marriage, shall he not diminish. And if he do not these three unto her, then shall she go out free without money.

This passage explains the laws regarding female slaves, servants, bondmaids, and handmaidens. The common explanation for a concubine is that she was a slave wife or a secondary wife; as we'll see, however, that's completely untrue. The context of these verses mentions slavery. Verse 7 notes that she doesn't go out free like the male slaves do. To say verse 7 deals with wives is to say verse 2 deals with husbands, not male slaves. Verse 8 says that if she falls out of favor, her master for whatever reason can sell her, provided that she isn't pledged to a husband, but not to any foreigners. If this passage described a wife, why would verse 7 have to state she cannot go free? Common sense dictates that Exodus 21 discusses laws related to slavery; that she can be redeemed (bought) further proves this. Does this mean a wife can be sold? There isn't one verse that supports this belief; if this were the case, you'd think the Pharisees would have been selling their wives, not divorcing them. It's also necessary to point out that a woman could be pledged to be a slave much like she could be pledged to be a wife. Context is key, which is why verse 8 makes such a distinction.

Exodus 21 also mentions that if a man buys her for his son, he should treat her like a daughter-in-law; she is also entitled to food, clothing, and shelter. Some translations say "conjugal rights" or "marriage rights," but the Hebrew word used is *ownah*, which appears only once in scripture, so determining what exactly it is referring to is hard. By comparing scripture with scripture, however, we are able to arrive at an answer that is consistent with *shelter* being the right word. If she is deprived of any one of these things, she can go free and is no longer a slave.

Leviticus 19:20 also deals with a female slave, also commonly referred to as a concubine. "And whosoever lieth carnally with a woman that is a bondmaid [*shiphchah*], betrothed to an husband [*iysh*], and not at all redeemed nor freedom given her: she shall be scourged; they shall not be put to death, because she was not free." The standard line from most Christians is that a concubine is a secondary wife or slave wife; but after reading this passage, it's impossible to argue that a woman can simultaneously be a man's slave and wife. We will see from other scriptures that this isn't the case. The Hebrew word *shipchah* is translated as "bondmaid"; it means "servant" or "slave." The word "husband" is translated from the Hebrew word *iysh* and should be translated "man." "Betrothed" is from the word *charaph* and literally means "to surrender to." The penalty for adultery was death for the woman and the man she had sex with (Exod. 20:14; Lev. 18:20; Deut. 5:18).

Leviticus 19:20 actually says that a woman who was a slave pledged or surrendered to a man couldn't have sex with any other person without her master's consent. If she were to do so, she and her partner would be punished but not put to death. This violation didn't bring the death penalty, but it was still a sin requiring a trespass offering to atone for their sin.

This scripture alone should end any argument from those who tout the secondary or slave-wife theory. God isn't the author of confusion, especially on issues regarding sexual sins. It's impossible for a wife to be a slave because she is a free woman—which is why, when she had sex with a man other than her husband, she was put to death for adultery. A female slave, on the other hand, wasn't redeemed; she was in bondage. And she could be punished but not be put to death because she wasn't free.

Saying a woman could be a slave wife is like saying a woman could be half pregnant; people who believe this nonsense are probably unaware of the deeper spiritual things in God's Word. If someone believes such a ridiculous doctrine, he or she more than likely doesn't understand that mankind is in bondage to sin but that believers have been redeemed through Jesus and are free. Believers represent the *ecclesia*, who are symbolically pledged to be the bride of Christ, while unbelievers continue to be slaves to sin. The author doesn't believe any Christians would say they are free in Christ and in bondage to sin at the same time; scripture doesn't teach this. Why do so many Christians continue to teach the secondary wife or slave-wife theory when God clearly made distinctions in his Word between concubines and wives?

We've already gone into exhaustive detail about the law in relation to divorce and remarriage; earlier in this chapter, we saw that Exodus 21:7–11 refers to slavery, not to marriage or divorce. There's no need for us to go into detail again on this scripture, except to state that it unquestionably speaks about a slave, not a wife. The reason why so many people stubbornly stick to a belief that is so contrary to the scriptures is this: if they say concubines aren't wives, then the men who had sex with them were doing so outside of wedlock. So they stick with their man-made traditions over God's law.

Even if you were to press the more reasonable-minded Christians, who incorrectly believe all sex outside of marriage is a sin, some would admit that concubines are a gray area. Joseph Bryant Rotherham's *Emphasized Bible* has a footnote for Leviticus 19:20, which says "given up to" or "legally secured to another man."[2] This is the more accurate translation of the verse, one that shouldn't be confined to a footnote. The problem is that many translators are in reality mere interpreters of God's Word, and their preconceived notions take priority over scripture, so they just rearrange things to fit their own bias.

Let us expound a little more on Exodus 21:10–11, which states, "If he take him another wife; her food, her raiment, and her duty of marriage, shall he not diminish. And if he do not these three unto her,

Sex Outside of Wedlock and Rape

then shall she go out free without money." The phrase "duty of marriage" is from the Hebrew word *ownah* and appears only this one time throughout scripture. The context, not the translators, should define the word, and the context refers to a slave, not a wife. The Septuagint uses the word "companionship"; either way it's difficult to determine the meaning of a word that occurs only once. The author is of the belief that *ownah*, which is defined as "dwell together," should be translated "shelter" since a similar word, *me'ownah*, is defined as "den, abode, and cohabitation." Let's read the Septuagint version of the laws dealing with a female slave.

> And if any one lie carnally with a woman, and she should be a home-servant kept for a man, and she has not been ransomed, and her freedom has not been given to her, they shall be visited with punishment; but they shall not die, because she was not set at liberty. (Lev. 19:20)

> And if any one sell his daughter as a domestic, she shall not depart as the maid-servants depart. If she be not pleasing to her master, after she has betrothed herself to him, he shall let her go free; but he is not at liberty to sell her to a foreign nation, because he has trifled with her. And if he should have betrothed her to his son, he shall do to her according to the right of daughters. And if he take another to himself, he shall not deprive her of necessaries and her apparel, and her companionship with him. And if he will not do these three things to her, she shall go out free without money. (Exod. 21:7–11)

A lot of people assume that "companionship" means marriage or sex, but the context says otherwise; "concubine" in English literally means "to cohabitate with." So the fact that the Greek Old Testament says "companionship" means that her master was to make sure she was taken care of and not neglected. If she was cohabitating with him on his property, he gave her the necessary companionship. Companionship can be an intimate friend, associate, or even an acquaintance; it certainly can't mean "conjugal rights," as some Bibles put it. This is because slaves weren't able to get married, so they had no right to sex. Let's back up to understand the proper context of scripture.

> If thou buy an Hebrew servant, six years he shall serve: and in the seventh he shall go out free for nothing. If he came in by himself, he shall go out by himself: if he were married, then his wife shall go out with him. If his master have given him a wife [*ishshah*], and she have born him sons or daughters; the wife and her children shall be her master's, and he shall go out by himself. And if the servant shall plainly say, I love my master, my wife, and my children; I will not go out free: Then his master shall bring him unto the judges; he shall also bring him to the door, or unto the door post; and his master shall bore his ear through with an aul; and he shall serve him for ever. (Exod. 21:2–6)

An honest reading of the preceding verses further clarifies that Exodus 7:11 doesn't grant any type of marriage duty or conjugal rights to a female slave. A man who owned a female slave or concubine could give her to one of his male slaves to breed more slaves, or he could sell her to someone else, provided he wasn't a foreigner, or he could have sex with her if he wanted to. The important point to remember is that she wasn't entitled to sex like a wife; neither was she limited to have sex with one man like a wife. Her master could have sex with her and four months later order her to have sex with a male slave he'd just acquired.

If a friend came to town, he could offer his concubine to his friend as a form of hospitality; on the flip side, a man could purchase a female slave or concubine and give her to his wife as a servant. He could also have sex with her or order her to have sex with another slave or friend. The scriptures also clearly state that if a male slave came in by himself, he would also leave the same way; thus, even if the master of a male slave gave him a female slave to have children with her, he wouldn't have been able to take them with him. This is because he went into bondage without a wife, so he couldn't be given a wife while he was in bondage. A female slave belonged to the master who purchased her; thus, she belonged to her master, not to the fellow male slave who had sex with her. She would still belong to her master long after the male slave who fathered her children was released. Exodus 21:4 uses the word "wife" for *ishshah*, but the context of scripture makes it clear that she wasn't a wife; the word should be translated "woman," since she didn't belong to a male slave—he was purchased just like she was. If she was a wife, he would have been able to take her with him when his enslavement ended. He couldn't do this if his master gave him a female slave to breed more slaves because she belonged to the man who had purchased her. When translators use the word "wife" instead of "woman," they contradict God's laws concerning marriage and adultery.

If Exodus 21:4 really says she was the wife of a male slave, given to him from his master, why did she still belong to her master and not to her "husband"? If her master had sex with her, let a friend have sex with her, let another male slave have sex with her, or allowed another male slave to have sex with her or to sell her, how would this activity not be considered adultery? You could let the context of scripture speak for itself and come to the understanding that she wasn't married to the male slave; she had sex with him out of wedlock. She wasn't free, so she couldn't be a wife while in bondage. No adultery took place because she wasn't married to anyone. Exodus 21:3 says that a man who was married and went into slavery left slavery married to his wife.

Abraham Hagar

Let's examine the relationship between Abraham, Sarah, and her servant Hagar by comparing scripture with scripture. After King Abimelech discovered from God that Sarah was Abraham's wife as well as his sister, he gave Abraham cattle, silver, and servants. This is according to Jasher 15:31. "And the king took a maiden whom he begat by his concubines, and he gave her to Sarai for a handmaid." God promised Abraham that he would be the father of many people, but Sarah was barren and past her childbearing years. Genesis 16:1–3 says,

> Now Sarai Abram's wife bare him no children: and she had an handmaid, an Egyptian, whose name was Hagar. And Sarai said unto Abram, Behold now, the Lord hath restrained me from bearing: I pray thee, go in unto my maid; it may be that I may obtain children by her. And Abram hearkened to the voice of Sarai. And Sarai Abram's wife took Hagar her maid the Egyptian, after Abram had dwelt ten years in the land of Canaan, and gave her to her husband Abram to be his wife.

Many Christians use the preceding verses to try to prove that Hagar married Abraham, but as we will see, Hagar never married him, and the phrase "to be his wife" is simply a euphemism for Abraham's having sex with Hagar. Sarah wanted to obtain children through Hagar; any offspring would belong to her, not Hagar. Sarah later despised Hagar because she conceived and bore Ishmael. Sarah would lay the blame on Abraham, even though having a child through Hagar was Sarah's idea from the start.

So what was Abraham's response to Sarah's complaints? Much like when he told Abimelech that Sarah was his sister, but not telling him she was also his wife, he'd left her vulnerable to his advances; Abraham abdicated his role as patriarch and told her Hagar was in her hand (Gen. 16:6). Abraham knew, or must have been at least suspicious, of the friction between Sarah and Hagar, yet he told Sarah that Hagar was her servant and to do with her what she liked. This led to a jealous Sarah, who afflicted Hagar to the point that Hagar ran away. And just like when Pharaoh took Sarah into his harem, God supernaturally interceded in the absence of Abraham's leadership. An angel of the Lord met Hagar and told her to go back and submit to her mistress. He also told her to name her son Ishmael because God had heard her affliction (Gen. 16:11). These verses are further proof that Hagar wasn't married to Abraham, but she remained Sarah's slave.

Abraham told Sarah that "thy maid is in your hand." If she had been his wife, he wouldn't have made such a comment. In fact, she was Sarah's possession. The angel of the Lord told Hagar to submit to her mistress, not to her husband, because she wasn't married; if Hagar had been married, Sarah wouldn't have been able to afflict her in the first place. You won't find any evidence in God's Word of a wife being a slave and taking orders from her sister wife; this was done only to slaves because they were in bondage. Wives were free.

Those who say Hagar was married based on Genesis 16:3 have a weak argument, to say the least. Genesis 25:12 says, "Now these are the generations of Ishmael, Abraham's son, whom Hagar the Egyptian, Sarah's handmaid, bare unto Abraham." One must ignore the weight of scripture, which testifies that Hagar was a slave, not a wife of Abraham.

Genesis 25:1 mentions Keturah for the first time and records, "Then again Abraham took a wife, and her name was Keturah." If wives can be called concubines and vice versa, why is it that Sarah was never described as a concubine? We continue with Genesis 25:6: "But unto the sons of the concubines, which Abraham had." Abraham had other concubines, not other wives. Further evidence is found in 1 Chronicles 1:32, which states, "Now the sons of Keturah, Abraham's concubine." Keturah wasn't Abraham's wife but his slave, a concubine, someone Sarah never was or could have been. Isaac, the child of God's promise, was Abraham's only child not conceived in bondage. If concubines were secondary wives or slave wives, why was Keturah mentioned as a concubine when Abraham took her after Sarah died? Why wasn't she elevated to a "full" wife? Why was she a secondary wife or slave wife after Sarah passed away? How could Abraham have had a secondary wife while he didn't have a wife of full status? Wouldn't Keturah have automatically become a wife of full status? And if she did become one, why was she still described as a concubine in 1 Chronicles 1:32 and Genesis 25:6? The word "wife" in Genesis 25:1 simply means "woman." Abraham took a woman after Sarah died, and she was a concubine (1 Chron. 1:32). In the book of Galatians, Paul compared Hagar and Sarah in such a way that it makes it impossible to accept the belief that concubines were secondary wives or slave wives.

> For it is written, that Abraham had two sons, the one by a bondmaid, the other by a freewoman. But he who was of the bondwoman was born after the flesh; but he of the freewoman was by promise. Which things are an allegory: for these are the two covenants; the one from the mount Sinai, which gendereth to bondage, which is Agar. For this Agar is mount Sinai in Arabia, and answereth to Jerusalem which now is, and is in bondage with her children. But Jerusalem which is above is free, which is the mother of us all. For it is written, Rejoice, thou barren that bearest not; break forth and cry, thou that travailest not: for the desolate hath many more children than she which hath an husband. Now we, brethren, as Isaac was, are the children of promise. But as then he that was born after the flesh persecuted him that was born after the Spirit, even so it is now. Nevertheless what saith the scripture? Cast out the bondwoman and her son: for the son of the bondwoman shall not be heir with the son of the freewoman. So then, brethren, we are not children of the bondwoman, but of the free. (Gal. 4:22–31)

Paul could make this comparison between Hagar and Sarah because Hagar was a slave and was never married to Abraham. His fathering a child with her meant only that Ishmael was born in bondage and not in freedom. Sarah, on the other hand, wasn't a slave but a free woman—Abraham's wife and the mother of the child of the promise, Isaac, and spiritual believers in Christ. Hagar represents unbelievers and their bondage to sin; she could never have been the wife of Abraham or the mother of the children of the promise because she was a slave.

When people promote the theory that concubines are secondary wives or slave wives, they either are unaware of the spiritual meaning each woman represents or refuse to acknowledge the facts. For those of you who still think concubines are wives and slaves at the same time, consider

Sex Outside of Wedlock and Rape

this: Do you believe a believer can be in bondage? It's ridiculous to argue that concubines are neither free nor in slavery; it must be one or the other. When someone says concubines were slave wives, he or she literally means they were free slaves; this is an oxymoron, to say the least, and makes as much sense as saying "cruel kindness."

God married Israel; he didn't purchase a concubine. Jesus will marry the *ecclesia*; he won't purchase a slave. There is not, has not, and never will be a group of people who are "unbelieving believers" from a mother who was a "free slave." You are either one or the other—hot or cold, rich or poor, faithful or unfaithful. Laban deceived Jacob, who married Leah. Laban gave his slave Zilpah to his daughter for a handmaiden (Gen. 29:24). Jacob worked seven more years for Laban and married Rachel. Laban gave her his slave Bilhah for a handmaiden (Gen. 29:29). God saw that Leah was hated, so he opened her womb, and Rachel was unable to conceive (Gen. 29:31). Leah had already given Jacob four sons, and Rachel was still barren, so she gave Jacob her slave Bilhah to act as a surrogate mother (Gen. 30:3). After Rachel's handmaiden bore two sons, Leah gave Jacob her handmaiden Zilpah as a surrogate mother so she could have more children (Gen. 30:9). Leah's plea for more children was eventually answered. Genesis 30:17–18 says, "And God hearkened unto Leah, and she conceived, and bare Jacob the fifth son. And Leah said, God hath given me my hire, because I have given my maiden to my husband: and she called his name Issachar."

Here we have God answering the prayer of a woman who was married to a polygynist—a sororal one at that—who was also sleeping with his wives' two handmaidens, and God blessed Leah with more children. He also eventually opened Rachel's womb (Gen. 30:22). The phrase "take her to wife" is simply a euphemism for sex; if you don't believe this is the case, why are Zilpah and Bilhah never mentioned among the matriarchs? Zilpah and Bilhah were slaves and didn't have a choice to sleep with Jacob; nor did they exercise authority over the children they bore, since Leah and Rachel named the children.

Proponents of the secondary/slave-wife theory cannot logically explain why Hagar was referred to as belonging to Sarah if she was Abraham's wife. Why would God suggest that Abraham listen to his wife and send Hagar away if she was also his wife? We've already seen how God views divorce, and scripture doesn't even hint at any divorce between Hagar and Abraham. On the other hand, if she was simply a slave, she could be released, but to admit this also concedes that Abraham was engaged in extramarital sex, and many don't want to do that.

Some proponents of the secondary/slave-wife theory turn to the story of the Levite and the concubine. The story begins by telling us that a Levite's concubine ran away and "played the whore against him" (Judg. 19:3). It bears repeating that the "husband" in verse 3 can also be translated "man"; this might not sound right in English, but this wasn't originally written in English. It was written in Hebrew. He is also called her "husband" in Judges 20:4.

In Judges 19:5, 7, the Levite is referred to as the concubine's father's son-in-law, but the word for "son-in-law" is *chathan*, which is also translated as "made affinity" in 1 Kings 3:1 and 2 Chronicles 18:1. Of course, "affinity" means "kinship" or "relationship," so the Hebrew word *chathan* denotes a relationship that could be a political, marriage, or master/slave relationship, which is what the relationship was between the Levite and his concubine. One must always be cognizant of the time period and culture and not look at things in an anachronistic manner like so many do today. After he spent an extended stay with his slave's father, he packed up his belongings and headed home. He finally found a place to lodge for the night at an old man's house in Gibeah.

> Now as they were making their hearts merry, behold, the men of the city, certain sons of Belial, beset the house round about, and beat at the door, and spake to the master of the house, the old man, saying, Bring forth the man that came into thine house, that we may know him. And the man, the master of the house, went out unto them, and said unto them, Nay, my brethren, nay, I pray you, do not so wickedly; seeing that this man is come into mine house, do not this folly. Behold, here is my daughter a maiden, and his

concubine; them I will bring out now, and humble ye them, and do with them what seemeth good unto you: but unto this man do not so vile a thing. [25] But the men would not hearken to him: so the man took his concubine, and brought her forth unto them; and they knew her, and abused her all the night until the morning: and when the day began to spring, they let her go. Then came the woman in the dawning of the day, and fell down at the door of the man's house where her lord was, till it was light. [27] And her lord rose up in the morning, and opened the doors of the house, and went out to go his way: and, behold, the woman his concubine was fallen down at the door of the house, and her hands were upon the threshold. And he said unto her, Up, and let us be going. But none answered. Then the man took her up upon an ass, and the man rose up, and gat him unto his place. And when he was come into his house, he took a knife, and laid hold on his concubine, and divided her, together with her bones, into twelve pieces, and sent her into all the coasts of Israel. And it was so, that all that saw it said, There was no such deed done nor seen from the day that the children of Israel came up out of the land of Egypt unto this day: consider of it, take advice, and speak your minds. (Josh. 19:22–30)

This story more accurately portrays the role of a concubine and confirms she was a slave. After erroneously referring to him as her "husband," the translators translated *iysh* as "man" in verse 25, and in verse 27 the Hebrew word *adown* is used. It is translated "lord" but can also mean "owner." The reason why he was called her lord or owner was that she was his slave, and while it's true that Sarah spoke to Abraham, calling him "lord" or "master," this wasn't in the master/slave sense. Paul also said Sarah was free, while Hagar was in bondage. In addition, how could a slave own another slave? The angel of the Lord told Hagar to go back and submit to her master.

The problem with the story of the Levite and the concubine is that few Christians dare to even address this story, and the ones who have the courage to do so are way off the mark. Scripture doesn't say the Levite was an important man, as some claim. If this were the case, why was he not even named? Another misconception is that he was a polygynist, but we aren't told whether he was even married; we're just told he owned a concubine and one male servant. The biggest misconception people have from this story is that the concubine should have been stoned to death for adultery. Leviticus 19:20, however, refutes this belief. It states that she should have been punished, along with her lover, but not put to death.

When the angry mob wanted the old man to bring out the Levite so they could rape him, the old man refused but offered his virgin daughter and the Levite's concubine. The mob, however, wouldn't even listen to him. So the Levite brought out his concubine, whom the mob abused and killed. He was able to do this because she was his slave, not his wife. This story is not unlike Lot's situation when he lived in Sodom; he offered his daughters, but not his wife, to the mob.

The Levite gave the mob his slave without asking for her consent because slaves don't have consent. The sin that occurred in this story was that the mob demanded sodomy, and they abused and killed his concubine. God's law does have certain limited rights, but outside those rights, slaves must obey their masters, and they have no consent.

Deuteronomy 21:10–14 says,

> When thou goest forth to war against thine enemies, and the Lord thy God hath delivered them into thine hands, and thou hast taken them captive, And seest among the captives a beautiful woman, and hast a desire unto her, that thou wouldest have her to thy wife; Then thou shalt bring her home to thine house; and she shall shave her head, and pare her nails; And she shall put the raiment of her captivity from off her, and shall remain in thine house, and bewail her father and her mother a full month: and after that thou shalt go in unto her, and be her husband, and she shall be thy wife. And it shall be, if thou have no delight in her, then thou shalt let her go whither she will; but thou shalt not sell her at all for money, thou shalt not make merchandise of her, because thou hast humbled her.

Sex Outside of Wedlock and Rape

Many have mistakenly interpreted this passage as regulating a so-called captive wife; in reality there is no marriage involved here, and "captive wife" is another oxymoron, since a captive is a prisoner or slave. There was no consent involved on the part of the woman who had been captured during warfare. It didn't matter to her captor whether she liked him or whether she wanted to live with him; she was a slave. For years Christians have either ignored this law or sugarcoated it by calling it a "marriage," when in fact many of these proponents know the Hebrew words for "wife" and "husband" could have differing meanings, depending on the context of scripture. The context here is clear; she was a captive—a slave held against her will—which is why the law stated she couldn't be sold to someone else. The reason for this is that she was captured as a slave and had a lifestyle that was against her will; she had suffered enough, so she was simply released from bondage.

In their vain attempt to make God more palatable to contemporary culture, apologists say that God commanded the woman to cut her nails and shave her head because he wanted the woman to be unattractive to her captor. Then he wouldn't want to keep her. The presumption is that God is so weak that he simply couldn't forbid Israelite soldiers from taking a woman captive. Those who still insist on this being a marriage and not a relationship outside of wedlock run into some key problems. First, there was no consent on the part of the woman, so they are left saying this was a "forceful-consent" relationship. Second, if this was a marriage, this detail must be inferred because scripture doesn't state marriage or divorce. If the argument is made that he could have sent her away in the "divorce" for no longer having delight in her, then they are left with the fact that there was no divorce for "just cause," since these same people claim Jesus allowed divorce in the New Testament. Whoever holds this view is left with a man having no delight in a woman, and that was just cause to divorce her, or Jesus was a liar, and the man could have divorced her for any reason.

These are the problems people face when they deviate from what the scriptures clearly state; instead of trying to be politically correct, we should employ an objective approach to scripture at all times. The best example of the law of the captive woman is when Moses commanded Israel to kill all the Midianites except the virgins, whom they could keep for themselves (Num. 31:17–18). Most contradictions are the result of people's flawed doctrinal beliefs and their determination to make scripture culturally relevant.

Sarah gave Hagar to Abraham for sex; the same situation happened when Jacob's wife Rachel gave him her slave Bilhah and Jacob's other wife Leah gave him her slave Zilpah. For all we know, Hagar, Bilhah, and Zilpah could have thought Jacob and Abraham were the ugliest men alive. Even if they found them attractive, that doesn't mean they wanted to have sex with them, but since they were slaves, they had no choice.

Unfortunately, political correctness has a dumbing-down effect on people. They can't seem to grasp that slaves belonged to their masters and had no control over themselves. Paul told believers, who were slaves, to obey their earthly masters; this would have included masters who wanted sex from their slaves (Eph. 6:5). In the law of the captive woman (erroneously called "captive wife"), Jacob, his concubines, and Abraham and Hagar demonstrated that a slave was in bondage and had no right to refuse a master; it also means they didn't have a right to have sex. This is further proof that the Hebrew word *ownah* doesn't mean "duty of marriage" or "conjugal rights"; Jacob had been cohabitating with Bilhah and Zilpah for years before he started having sex with them; the same is true of Hagar and Abraham. In both cases the concubines were provided with food, clothing, and shelter. This is in keeping with the law established in Exodus 21:10.

Let's return to the matter of King David and his adultery and subsequent murder of Uriah. God cursed him by saying,

> Thus saith the Lord, Behold, I will raise up evil against thee out of thine own house, and I will take thy wives [*ishshah*] before thine eyes, and give them unto thy neighbour, and he shall lie with thy wives

[*ishshah*] in the sight of this sun. For thou didst it secretly: but I will do this thing before all Israel, and before the sun. (2 Sam. 12:11–12)

David got word that his son Absalom had planned a coup against his own father and fled for his life. Second Samuel 15:16 says, "And the king went forth, and all his household after him. And the king left ten women [*ishshah*], which were concubines, to keep the house." Obviously, if David had known he was fulfilling prophecy, he wouldn't have left his concubines to keep the house. But if concubines are wives, why didn't he leave all his wives behind? Why didn't he take all his wives with him, and why is there a distinction between concubines and wives? It should be clear that the concubines weren't wives but merely slaves David had left behind to keep the house. David wasn't even sure whether he would be able to return to Israel, whether it be from death or exile (2 Sam. 15:25–26). When people mention God's telling David that another man would sleep with his "wives" as proof that concubines were wives, they are grasping at straws because the Hebrew word for "wives" in 2 Samuel 12:11 simply means "women." That they are women called concubines in 2 Samuel 15:16, 16:21–22 confirms this.

With his father, David, fleeing for his life, Absalom obtained advice from Ahithophel, one of David's counselors. Second Samuel 16:21 says, "And Ahithophel said unto Absalom, Go in unto thy father's concubines, which he hath left to keep the house; and all Israel shall hear that thou art abhorred of thy father: then shall the hands of all that are with thee be strong." Absalom decided to act on Ahithophel's advice and proceeded to fulfill prophecy. Second Samuel 16:22 says, "So they spread Absalom a tent upon the top of the house; and Absalom went in unto his father's concubines in the sight of all Israel."

If concubines were wives, then Absalom's reign wouldn't have had so many Israelites on his side, considering that adultery carried the death penalty and that many witnessed this public act. People who don't want to admit that concubines weren't wives simply ignore these facts.

The Lord was with David after all, and he returned to his house in Jerusalem after the defeat and the death of Absalom and his men. Second Samuel 20:3 says,

> And David came to his house at Jerusalem; and the king took the ten women his concubines, whom he had left to keep the house, and put them in ward, and fed them, but went not in unto them. So they were shut up unto the day of their death, living in widowhood.

Those who stubbornly cling to the notion that concubines are wives run into numerous problems; based on their interpretation of Exodus 21:10–11, David lived out the remainder of his life in willful sin before God since these women were entitled to sex. If they were his wives and they had sex with Absalom, then they needed to be stoned to death for adultery. Defenders of the secondary/slave-wife definition of concubinage say David was still guilty about his own adultery and therefore didn't put them to death; but if this is the case, they would still have been entitled to sex given that they were still alive and married to him. Others say Absalom raped David's concubines, which resulted in David's not having sex with them, because they were defiled; the problem with this belief is that nowhere does God say men were to withhold sex from their wives if they were raped. The argument that Absalom raped David's concubines is rather weak; the scriptures state that Absalom had many people on his side, and when you add the fact that David took his wives and fled from Jerusalem, many people had no problem serving their new King Absalom.

Absalom's new supporters included one of David's own closest advisers, Ahithophel, so it should be of no surprise if David's concubines were more than willing to show their loyalty to the new king by having sex with him. When one compares scripture with scripture and discards preconceived ideas, it becomes clear why David acted the way he did to his concubines. David didn't have his concubines put to death because they weren't his wives; therefore, they hadn't committed adultery with Absalom. However, they were guilty of sin, since these concubines were David's slaves and could be punished according to Leviticus 19:20. David chose to punish his concubines by never having sex with them again, keeping them in "widowhood." David still provided for them by placing them in a ward and giving them clothing and food; this is everything a female slave was entitled to, according to Exodus 21:10. Those who insist that concubines were wives of lesser rank must somehow reconcile David's action with the fact that he did what was right in the Lord's eyes except for his sins regarding Uriah and Bathsheba (1 Kings 15:5). God chastises those he loves, which is why he punished David for taking the census and committing murder and adultery; however; there was no punishment for David's treatment of his concubines because he did no wrong. If one views concubines as wives, then he or she cannot arrive at this simple explanation.

All that remains now are a few miscellaneous passages that appear to condemn unmarried sex. First Corinthians 7:2 says, "Nevertheless, to avoid fornication, let every man have his own wife, and let every woman have her own husband." It's important to take what Paul said in context. In the preceding verse, Paul said, "Now concerning the things whereof ye wrote unto me: It is good for a man not to touch a woman."

Paul gave his opinion on the matter of marriage; this is what he meant by saying "touch" and why he used "nevertheless" to begin verse 2. Every man should have a wife, Paul said, and every woman should have a husband to avoid *porneia*. This is nothing more than Paul's own opinion, and it's a rather weak one at that when you consider the fact that many Christians read into the text that pornography and masturbation, in addition to unmarried sex, are included in *porneia*. In other words, a man who is "sinning" by masturbating should avoid further "sins" in this regard by marrying a woman. How many Christians who believe masturbation, unmarried sex, and pornography are *porneia* actually teach this? As stated earlier, pornography is a sin only if it is an addiction, so the solution for a man's suffering from this "sin" is to get married?

Paul's advice for illicit sex (*porneia*) also logically includes giving a homosexual a heterosexual spouse as a solution to a much deeper spiritual problem. Paul went on to give his opinion on other matters as well (1 Cor.

7:6). He even said it's better to be single like himself than to be married (1 Cor. 7:7–8). He made it clear, however, when he was giving a commandment of the Lord that must be obeyed (1 Cor. 7:10). Getting involved in a serious covenant, such as marriage, isn't something that should be done just because one masturbates or has unmarried sex, neither of which are sins anyway. First Corinthians 7:2 is just more proof of circular reasoning done on the part of the so-called puritanical "purity" crowd. What's to stop the author from using this same logic and say men and women should kiss each other only within marriage and that those who fail to do so are committing fornication (*porneia*)? Those who say romantic kissing isn't sin but that masturbation and pornography are cannot make a scriptural defense of excluding kissing from such a list. The only times people romantically kissed each other in scripture outside of marriage were in the Song of Solomon, and we have already seen that they also had sex before marriage. Jacob's kissing Rachel was simply done as a greeting when they first met each other, so unless one submits to the scripture-by-scripture method employed in this book and uses the Old Testament to interpret the New, one cannot make a solid scriptural case for romantic kissing being lawful or unlawful between unmarried persons.

Most people who use New Testament verses to "prove" unmarried sex is a sin employ eisegesis and just simply assume that unmarried sex is *porneia* and therefore a sin. Hebrews 13:4 says, "Marriage is honorable in all, and the bed undefiled: but whoremongers [*pornos*] and adulterers God will judge." The Greek word *pornos* is defined as "prostitute" in addition to "whoremonger" and "fornicator." It should be rather easy to discern what *pornos* means in this verse by employing sound exegesis. God doesn't forbid secular or common prostitution, nor does he forbid unmarried sex. The conclusion here is that *pornos* refers to sacred prostitution or sexual idolatry, a view consistent with the Old Testament, which should always be used to interpret the New Testament.

Second Corinthians 12:21 says, "And lest, when I come again, my God will humble me among you, and that I shall bewail many which have sinned already, and have not repented of the uncleanness and fornication and lasciviousness which they have committed." "Uncleanness" simply means "impurity." Any sin considered impure (and *porneia*) is defined as illicit sex. Unmarried sex isn't a sin; therefore, it isn't impure. It also isn't illicit because no shedding of blood was required. It also doesn't violate any fruit of the Spirit.

> The elder women as mothers; the younger as
> sisters, with all purity. (1 Tim. 5:2)

> To be discreet, chaste, keepers at home, good, obedient to their own husbands, that the word of God be not blasphemed. (Titus 2:5)

> While they behold your chaste conversation
> coupled with fear. (1 Pet. 3:2)

When Christians remove their anachronistic lenses, a clear view of scripture appears; for a man or woman to be pure or clean, he or she would have to live a sin-free life. A virgin who is an unbeliever isn't pure but is rather impure due to sin. On the other hand, a believer who is a prostitute is pure because purity is based on obedience to God's laws. Titus 2:5 should be sufficient proof for anyone that being chaste or pure has nothing to do with virginity and everything to do with obeying God's law. It should be clear that Christian wives are called to be chaste in the sense of being sin-free, not of abstaining from sex. Abstinence isn't allowed in marriages except for fasting for a limited time (1 Cor. 7:5).

The fruit of the Spirit—love, joy, peace, longsuffering, gentleness, goodness, faith, meekness, and temperance—also help to define what sin is in addition to the law revealed in the Old Testament. Another argument against unmarried sex could include condemning it as a sin based on lack of temperance or self-control. The reason Christians cannot engage in sex outside of marriage is that it means they lack self-control and can't wait for marriage. Those who argue this way mistakenly or purposefully conflate abstinence with self-control. A man can choose to abstain from alcohol, and another man can choose not to. But does this mean the man who chooses not to lacks self-control? He would lack self-control only if he were an alcoholic; likewise, a couple who chooses to engage in unmarried sex is compared to another couple who chooses to wait until marriage. Not waiting doesn't mean they lack self-control. Not abstaining from something doesn't mean you lack self-control. A couple could lack self-control and be addicted to sex within a monogamous marriage.

Some people often mention the woman at the well in regard to either divorce and remarriage or sex outside of wedlock. As we will read, however, this is yet another biblical misconception from which too many Christians have gleaned incorrect doctrine.

> Jesus saith unto her, Go, call thy husband, and come hither. The woman answered and said, I have no husband. Jesus said unto her, Thou hast well said, I have no husband: For thou hast had five husbands; and he whom thou now hast is not thy husband: in that saidst thou truly The woman saith unto him, Sir, I perceive that thou art a prophet. (John 4:16–19)

Nowhere does Jesus condemn this woman for any sin because she hadn't committed any, even though she was "shacking up" with a man. We can also ascertain from the scriptures that the woman by the well wasn't divorced from five men because as we've already seen, Jesus taught that divorce and remarriage is adultery. To say that he approved of divorce renders his teachings in the synoptic Gospels nonsensical. Jesus said she'd had five husbands, meaning past tense. If her first husband had still been alive, he wouldn't have said she had five husbands but that she had only one and was committing adultery. Jesus demonstrated that in addition to being the Messiah, he was also a prophet. He didn't tell her to get married or move out; nor did he tell her to go and sin no more. The woman at the well didn't show any regret or remorse for doing anything wrong, unlike others such as Zacchaeus (Luke 19:8). She was so excited that she left her water pot behind and went into the city to tell everyone, "Come, see a man, which told me all things that ever I did: is not this the Christ?" (John 4:29).

It isn't difficult to assume that each of her five husbands had died; the Sadducees, who quote the Apocrypha, Tobit 3:8 (Matt. 22:25–27) when they tested Jesus on the resurrection, made such a case. So it isn't out of the question that the woman at the well was in a similar situation, since widowhood was more common then than it is nowadays. Even if one were to reject the theory that she was a five-time widow, the following facts cannot be denied:

1. She was living with a man she wasn't married to.
2. Jesus didn't command her to marry him or separate.
3. If one insists that she was married, then he or she must account for Jesus's teachings related to divorce and remarriage, stated earlier.

The word "whoredom" can refer to something that may or may not be a sin. Depending on the Bible version, it could be "harlotry," "fornication," or "sexual immorality"—*zanah* in Hebrew or *porneia* in Greek. Prostitution is definitely whoredom, fornication, and harlotry; but as long as it's not sacred prostitution or sexual idolatry, no sin is being committed. The same applies to two unmarried people having sex; they are committing whoredom, but they aren't sinning. Not all *zanah* or *porneia* is sin. One must pay attention to the context.

John 8:41 says, "We be not born of fornication; we have one Father, even God." Here the Pharisees insisted that Jesus was born outside of wedlock; of course, the Pharisees were incorrect. However, from that verse we can deduce that being born outside of wedlock qualified as *porneia*; Jephthah is a good example of being born of whoredom or fornication. As we've already learned, he was the son of a prostitute, so this whoredom wasn't a sin. Compare this to David's son; he was conceived with Bathsheba, which was also whoredom, but it was sin because it was an adulterous relationship.

In short, unmarried sex isn't a sin unless it violates God's other laws. The concubines spoken of in the Bible weren't secondary or slave wives but simply slaves, and having unauthorized sex with them wasn't considered adultery but definitely sinful. When men engaged in lawful sex with a concubine or prostitute, it constituted unmarried sex, which can also be considered whoredom (*zanah*) or fornication (*porneia*). It's important to look at the context to determine whether whoredom or fornication denotes a lawful or unlawful act. The following are just some of the men of God who engaged in lawful, unmarried sex (whoredom, fornication):

Caleb had two concubines (1 Chron. 2:46–48).

Rehoboam had sixty concubines (2 Chron. 11:21).

Abraham had concubines (Gen. 25:6).

Jacob had two concubines, Bilhah and Zilpah (Gen. 30:1–9).

Abraham's brother Nahor had a concubine (Gen. 22:24).

Eliphaz had the concubine, Timma (Gen. 36:12).

David had ten concubines (2 Sam. 15:16).

RAPE

The book of Deuteronomy deals with laws regarding rape, with explanations on how to punish the rapist based on the status of the woman involved. Most Bible stories people consider to be about rape are assumptions in which people infer rape took place, but the scriptures are silent.

> [23] If a damsel that is a virgin be betrothed unto an husband, and a man find her in the city, and lie with her; Then ye shall bring them both out unto the gate of that city, and ye shall stone them with

stones that they die; the damsel, because she cried not, being in the city; and the man, because he hath humbled [*anah*] his neighbour's wife: so thou shalt put away evil from among you. [25] But if a man find a betrothed damsel in the field, and the man force [*chazaq*] her, and lie with her: then the man only that lay with her shall die: But unto the damsel thou shalt do nothing; there is in the damsel no sin worthy of death: for as when a man riseth against his neighbour, and slayeth him, even so is this matter: For he found her in the field, and the betrothed damsel cried, and there was none to save her. [28] If a man find a damsel that is a virgin, which is not betrothed, and lay hold [*taphas*] on her, and lie with her, and they be found; Then the man that lay with her shall give unto the damsel's father fifty shekels of silver, and she shall be his wife; because he hath humbled (*anah*) her, he may not put her away all his days. (Deut. 22:23–29)

The preceding chapter actually begins with adultery, and both parties were put to death. Then it continues in verse 23 to describe the adultery of a woman pledged to be married, but she didn't cry out for help, so the act wasn't considered rape. Both parties were put to death. Notice that verse 25 deals with a man who raped a woman pledged to be married to another man—this is rape of a married woman, and the perpetrator was put to death for adultery. The woman was left alone because she was raped. The Hebrew word *chazaq* is used to denote "force"; unfortunately, many Christians fail to grasp that the man was put to death for adultery, not for rape. The woman wasn't put to death because she was forced against her will to commit adultery, so she was blameless. The biggest obstacle, which many Christians try to shy away from, is verse 28, which describes an unmarried woman who was raped, but the perpetrator wasn't put to death. Instead he simply had to marry her. To work around this issue, which many Christians find embarrassing in modern society, they insist that *taphas*, which is translated "lay hold," implies consensual sex. But a simple search of the word *taphas* should be enough to quell any lingering doubts.

And she caught [*taphas*] him by his garment…[Potiphar's wife attempting to have sex with Joseph.] (Gen. 39:12)

And a man lie with her carnally, and it be hid from the eyes of her husband, and be kept close, and she be defiled and there be no witness against her, neither she be taken [*taphas*]. (Num. 5:13)

Then shall his father and mother lay hold [*taphas*] on him, and bring him out unto the elders of his city. (Deut. 21:19)

And it shall be when you have taken [*taphas*] the city. (Josh. 8:8)

And the king of Ai they took [*taphas*] alive. (Josh. 8:23)

And he took [*taphas*] Agag the King of the Amalekites. (1 Sam. 15:8)

And Elijah said unto them, Take [*taphas*] the prophets. (1 Kings 18:40)

And he said, Whether they be come out for peace, take [*taphas*] them alive. (1 Kings 20:18)

Then said Jeremiah, It is false; I fall not away to the Chaldeans. But he hearkened not to him: so Irijah took [*taphas*] Jeremiah, and brought him to the princes. (Jer. 37:14)

Opponents insist *taphas* doesn't always mean taking hold of someone against his or her will. As proof to support their view, they cite verses like Ezekiel 27:29. The word *taphas* is translated "And all that handle [*taphas*] the oar" and in Genesis 4:21, where *taphas* is translated "of all such as handle [*taphas*] the harp and organ." This isn't a solid argument and only deflects from the real issue, which is that the story in question relates to *taphas* in relation to people, not to inanimate objects. A simple search for the word *taphas* reveals it isn't consensual but involves taking someone by force against his or her will. Numerous other verses confirm this truth; one can easily do his or her own study on this matter if doubts linger. There isn't one case in the Old Testament where the word *taphas* is used in a voluntary manner.

Genesis 34 tells us about Jacob's only daughter, Dinah, and her subsequent encounter with Shechem, which many assume was rape.

> And Dinah the daughter of Leah, which she bare unto Jacob, went out to see the daughters of the land. And when Shechem the son of Hamor the Hivite, prince of the country, saw her, he took [*laqach*] her, and lay with her, and defiled [*anah*] her. And his soul clave unto Dinah the daughter of Jacob, and he loved the damsel, and spake kindly unto the damsel. And Shechem spake unto his father Hamor, saying, Get me this damsel to wife. And Jacob heard that he had defiled Dinah his daughter: now his sons were with his cattle in the field: and Jacob held his peace until they were come. (Gen. 34:1–5)

Many have concluded that Shechem raped Dinah because of the word *anah*, which is translated as "defiled" in verse 2, but Deuteronomy 22:24 uses this same word to describe consensual sex between a woman pledged to be married and another man, both of whom were put to death for adultery. So the Hebrew word *anah* in verse 2 doesn't necessarily refer to rape, and the word *taphas* isn't used at all here; the word *laqach* is used instead. This word describes this encounter as ambiguous. Unlike *taphas*, which always denotes force, *laqach* could possibly denote the use of force. The story of Dinah and Shechem isn't as obvious as some people make it out to be. When one considers the fact that he cleaved to her, spoke kindly to her, and was called more honorable than anyone in his father's house (v. 19), it is hard to imagine that he raped Dinah.

We should also note that Shechem was willing to pay any dowry or gift after he had sex with (defiled) her; this would foreshadow the law that required a man to marry a virgin he had defiled unless the father refused.

Shechem and Hamor were willing to do everything written in the law to rectify the situation, and Jacob had the right to accept or refuse Dinah from getting married. While Jacob was still mulling things over, Simeon and Levi decided to undermine their father's authority in the affair by telling Hamor and Shechem to get everyone circumcised so he could marry Dinah. Getting circumcised as an adult is obviously not an easy task; Shechem was madly in love with Dinah and would have stood on his head if they'd asked him to.

Simeon and Levi used Hamor's household circumcision against them. They killed all the males, took the women and children captive, and looted the city (Gen. 34:25–29). In addition to not honoring their father by waiting for his response, they decided to kill, steal, and lie; and they took advantage of Shechem's desire to marry Dinah. Seemingly Jacob leaned toward allowing Dinah to marry Shechem because during the negotiations that transpired for days, maybe even a few weeks, Jacob never demanded that Shechem or Hamor return his daughter to him. She stayed in Shechem's house during the whole affair. When Simeon and Levi lied to Shechem and Hamor, they threatened to remove Dinah from his house if they didn't get circumcised. It's rather hard to believe that Jacob wouldn't have allowed Dinah to marry Shechem, yet he let her stay in his house. It is especially hard to understand if she was raped, as some Christians believe. When she was finally removed from his house and brought back, Jacob was angry at what his sons had done and was afraid of retaliation (Gen. 34:26–30). Genesis 34:31 says, "And they [Levi, Simeon] said, Should he [Shechem] deal with our sister as with an harlot?"

This statement Levi and Simeon made is ironic given the fact that they undermined their father's authority and that Shechem was trying to rectify the situation. They are the reason she was never mentioned as being married. Levi and Simeon used their sister as bait and never intended to allow her to marry Shechem. Jacob later cursed them for their actions (Gen. 49:5–7), a curse God honored (Josh. 19:1). Even if one were to insist that Shechem raped Dinah, the law didn't prescribe the death penalty (Deut. 22:28–29).

In closing, it is worth noting that the same people who infer Shechem raped Dinah don't make the same inference that David raped Bathsheba. Second Samuel 11:4 says, "And David sent messengers, and took her; and she came in unto him, and he lay with her; for she was purified from her uncleanness: and she returned unto her house." This text doesn't tell us whether she wanted to sleep with David; we aren't even told whether David loved her, for that matter. The point is, why don't the same people who infer Shechem raped Dinah make the same inference with David and Bathsheba?

Amnon and Tamar

In the case of Amnon and Tamar, we have absolute proof that a rape occurred. The scriptures leave no room for doubt or speculation. Second Samuel 13:1–16 says,

> And it came to pass after this, that Absalom the son of David had a fair sister, whose name was Tamar; and Amnon the son of David loved her. And Amnon was so vexed, that he fell sick for his sister Tamar; for she was a virgin; and Amnon thought it hard for him to do any thing to her. But Amnon had a friend, whose name was Jonadab, the son of Shimeah David's brother: and Jonadab was a very subtil man. And he said unto him, Why art thou, being the king's son, lean from day to day? wilt thou not tell me? And Amnon said unto him, I love Tamar, my brother Absalom's sister. And Jonadab said unto him, Lay thee down on thy bed, and make thyself sick: and when thy father cometh to see thee, say unto him, I pray thee, let my sister Tamar come, and give me meat, and dress the meat in my sight, that I may see it, and eat it at her hand. So Amnon lay down, and made himself sick: and when the king was come to see him, Amnon said unto the king, I pray thee, let Tamar my sister come, and make me a couple of cakes in my sight, that I may eat at her hand. Then David sent home to Tamar, saying, Go now to thy brother Amnon's house, and dress him meat. So Tamar went

to her brother Amnon's house; and he was laid down. And she took flour, and kneaded it, and made cakes in his sight, and did bake the cakes. And she took a pan, and poured them out before him; but he refused to eat. And Amnon said, Have out all men from me. And they went out every man from him. And Amnon said unto Tamar, Bring the meat into the chamber, that I may eat of thine hand. And Tamar took the cakes which she had made, and brought them into the chamber to Amnon her brother. [11] And when she had brought them unto him to eat, he took hold [*chazaq*] of her, and said unto her, Come lie with me, my sister. [12] And she answered him, Nay, my brother, do not force [*anah*] me; for no such thing ought to be done in Israel: do not thou this folly. And I, whither shall I cause my shame to go? and as for thee, thou shalt be as one of the fools in Israel. Now therefore, I pray thee, speak unto the king; for he will not withhold me from thee. [14] Howbeit he would not hearken unto her voice: but, being stronger [*chazaq*] than she, forced [*anah*] her, and lay with her. Then Amnon hated her exceedingly; so that the hatred wherewith he hated her was greater than the love wherewith he had loved her. And Amnon said unto her, Arise, be gone. And she said unto him, There is no cause: this evil in sending me away is greater than the other that thou didst unto me. But he would not hearken unto her.

In verse 14 the word "stronger" is translated from the word *chazaq*, the same word used for the raped, betrothed woman in Deuteronomy 22:25; the word "forced" is the Hebrew word *anah*, which is a proper translation given Tamar didn't consent to this act. There can be no doubt that this act of evil Amnon did was rape; Tamar appealed to Deuteronomy 22:28–29, confirming that it was written for a raped, unpledged virgin such as herself. She even stated that having her removed was more evil than the act itself (v. 16).

Anyone arguing that Deuteronomy 22:28–29 doesn't refer to rape is left with the scenario of there being no law against rape of an unpledged virgin, or that all sex outside of marriage is rape; but a concise reading of the scriptures doesn't support this view. There was no law regarding the rape of an unmarried single woman; however, this doesn't mean doing so isn't a sin, since such an act is a violation of the fruit of the Spirit. Obviously, any man who claims he loves his neighbor and then rapes her is a liar and neither loves nor respects the victim. A rapist isn't someone who is kind, gentle, or loving toward his or her neighbor. The fact that the law mentions punishment only for limited types of rape doesn't mean the other types not mentioned aren't sin; greed, drunkenness, and envy are not specifically mentioned in the law either. But we know that any violation of the fruit of the Spirit is a sin against God, and we should never forget this important fact.

CHAPTER 5

Anal Sex

WE NOW APPROACH THE SUBJECT of sodomy, which is defined in this work as anal sex. If you're wondering why the word "sodomy" is used instead of "homosexuality," the reason will become clear by the end of this chapter. As always, we start from the Old Testament and work our way to the New Testament to discern what the scriptures really say in terms of sodomy.

> Thou shalt not lie [*shakab*] with mankind, as with
> womankind: it is abomination. (Lev. 18:22)

> If a man also lie [*shakab*] with mankind, as he lieth with a woman,
> both of them have committed an abomination: they shall surely
> be put to death; their blood shall be upon them. (Lev. 20:13)

We've already seen, based on the previous chapter, that the word *taphas* or *chazaq* is used to denote rape. However, *taphas* isn't found in either of these verses, unlike Deuteronomy 22:28, so we know no one was being taken against his will in terms of sodomy. Even though the word *shakab* is used of Amnon's rape of Tamar, clearly Tamar didn't want to have sex with her brother. So the word *chazaq* is used to describe his strength, which he used to force (*anah*) her (2 Sam. 13:14) and *shakab* (lie) with her. The word *anah*, which can mean "force" or "defiled," is also absent from these verses, so one must conclude then that God forbids all practices involving homosexual sodomy, not just homosexual rape.

Some homosexual proponents argue that the ban on sodomy was temporary and part of some so-called holiness code that also includes such activities as men cutting their beards or the sides of their hair, wearing mixed fabrics, touching unclean animals or unclean persons, and so forth. The fact is that there is no such thing as a "holiness code"; this is nothing more than a doctrine of man with no basis of support. One of the reasons sodomy has gained (and will continue to gain) ground is Christians' lack of understanding of what sin is and how to properly define it. No shedding of blood was required for men who didn't grow a beard, nor were they put to death for disobeying this command from God. It violates none of the fruit of the Spirit. Men were going bald then just as they are now, so we know that at least some men broke this law. The same can also be said of wearing mixed fabrics. As for touching anything or anyone unclean, the sin wasn't the act of touching; the sin was the failure to cleanse oneself after doing so. This is why God struck people dead—not when they touched something deemed unclean but when they refused to cleanse themselves as God had commanded in the law. Once again touching something God called unclean wasn't a sin, just a minor inconvenience.

These laws were intended only for God's physical temple, which no longer exists; he no longer resides in physical temples but in people—the first being his only begotten son and, since Pentecost, his believers. Unlike God's physical temple, if you touched Jesus, you would be made clean; you couldn't make him unclean (Luke 8:44). Also, people who believe homosexuality was part of a so-called holiness code fail to realize that Jesus said, "Think not that I am come to destroy the law or the prophets: I am not come to destroy, but to fulfill" (Matt. 5:17). It's also important to note that the so-called holiness code included bestiality, incest, and adultery. Are the laws against these sins no longer binding? What sets sodomy apart from wearing mixed fabrics? Adultery required the shedding of blood for sin; wearing mixed fabrics was never a sin.

The Hebrew word for a sacred/temple prostitute isn't used in either of these verses; *qadesh* is nowhere to be found here. Some may argue that the context refers to sacred prostitution because God mentioned human sacrifice to Molech in verse 21; with this reasoning one would have to assume God forbade bestiality only in terms of worship to Molech. So nonreligious bestiality is OK? Why does God say the inhabitants defiled the land and that he would cast them out for committing these sins? When other tribes who worshipped other gods occupied the land, not everyone who practiced child sacrifice, bestiality, adultery, or sodomy did so for religious reasons, yet God said they'd defiled the land in doing so. One must conclude that the religious or nonreligious practices of child sacrifice and sodomy were what defiled the land (Lev. 18:24–25). Further proof that this condemns all homosexuality between men is that neither Molech nor any other god is mentioned in Leviticus 20:12 prior to the prohibition on sodomy in verse 13, as is the case of Leviticus 18:21, preceding the prohibition of sodomy in verse 22.

When it comes to lesbianism, many Christians are, in fact, surprised to know it isn't mentioned at all in the sexual prohibitions in Leviticus or in any other book for that matter; as mentioned earlier, sex is biblically defined as penile-vaginal penetration. It isn't possible for women to have sex with each other. The act of a woman strapping on a dildo and penetrating another woman doesn't count as sex; this also proves that oral sex isn't considered sex, given the fact that women can perform oral sex on each other.

> Thou shalt not lie with mankind, as with womankind: it is abomination. Neither shalt thou lie with any beast to defile thyself therewith: neither shall any woman stand before a beast to lie down thereto: it is confusion. (Lev. 18:22)

> If a man also lie with mankind, as he lieth with a woman, both of them have committed an abomination: they shall surely be put to death; their blood shall be upon them...And if a man lie with a beast, he shall surely be put to death: and ye shall slay the beast. And if a woman approach unto any beast, and lie down thereto, thou shalt kill the woman, and the beast: they shall surely be put to death; their blood shall be upon them. (Lev. 20:13, 15–16)

Notice that when God condemns male homosexuality, he is silent in regard to female homosexuality; the common argument is that when God prohibits male homosexuality, this principle extends to female homosexuality. The problem with this belief is that God goes out of his way to condemn male and female bestiality; had God not mentioned female bestiality, the argument could be made that the male homosexual and bestiality prohibitions extend to women. But given the fact that God mentioned female bestiality but not lesbianism disproves this theory. Biblically speaking, female homosexuality is an oxymoron; it simply doesn't exist. A woman cannot naturally vaginally penetrate another woman.

The problem is that many Christians commit eisegesis and assume oral sex is considered sex biblically, but the scriptures don't condemn oral sex (much like kissing), so they cannot make a solid biblical case for prohibiting lesbianism. Even if they were miraculously able to do so, they would still have to explain God's silence when he explicitly mentioned female bestiality. As a last resort, critics who believe lesbianism is sin appeal to Romans 1:26–27.

> [26] For this cause God gave them up unto vile affections: for even their women did change the natural use [*chresis*] into that which is against nature: [27] And likewise also the men, leaving the natural use [*chresis*] of the woman, burned in their lust one toward another; men with men working that which is unseemly, and receiving in themselves that recompence of their error which was meet.

The Greek word for "use," *chresis*, is only used in these two verses. In scripture it means "in a sexual sense" or "intercourse." Romans is where many Christians incorrectly believe lesbianism is a sin. But when one reads verse 26 closely, one realizes that Paul didn't say women with women; in verse 27 he actually said "men with men." Unfortunately, many Christians use the "men with men" of verse 27 to interpret verse 26; however, Paul actually stated that "their women did change the natural use into that which is against nature." Since Paul didn't say women with women, we can safely say that the women engaged in unnatural sex with men; that Paul said "likewise" in verse 27 when he mentioned "men with men" is further evidence. So Paul said that women engaged in unnatural sex with men and that men also engaged in unnatural sex with other men; the only conclusion we can come to is anal sex. Considering lawful sex is biblically defined as only penile-vaginal penetration, this is the only conclusion that makes sense.

Paul's condemnation of anal sex or sodomy is consistent with the prohibitions in the Old Testament; this also explains God's silence in regard to lesbianism in the sexual prohibitions listed in Leviticus 18 and 20. Ironically, many unbelievers mock Christianity for some of the things mentioned in scripture, while at the same time they believe women can have sex with each other, when scripture's silence speaks loudly to the fact that this isn't possible. One argument some Christians use is that lesbianism isn't explicitly condemned because of threesomes; the first polygynist Lamech more than likely engaged in the first threesome (there truly is nothing new under the sun); however, if this is the case, God would still have been able to condemn lesbianism without banning threesomes. Given the grouping of one man with two women, one shouldn't automatically assume that the two women are having sex with each other. Of course, this is a moot point because, as we've already seen, it's impossible for women to have sex with other women.

Instead of focusing on the fact that God's law prohibits heterosexual and homosexual sodomy, many focus on lesbianism, which isn't a sin. It's rather unfortunate to admit that some Christians teach that homosexual sodomy is forbidden but that heterosexual sodomy is allowed; such false doctrine makes a mockery of the scriptures and shows their lack of understanding of Romans 1:26.

Romans 1:18–32 says,

[18] For the wrath of God is revealed from heaven against all ungodliness and unrighteousness of men, who hold the truth in unrighteousness; [19] Because that which may be known of God is manifest in them; for God hath shewed it unto them. [20] For

the invisible things of him from the creation of the world are clearly seen, being understood by the things that are made, even his eternal power and Godhead; so that they are without excuse: [21] Because that, when they knew God, they glorified him not as God, neither were thankful; but became vain in their imaginations, and their foolish heart was darkened. [22] Professing themselves to be wise, they became fools, [23] And changed the glory of the uncorruptible God into an image made like to corruptible man, and to birds, and fourfooted beasts, and creeping things.

[24] Wherefore God also gave them up to uncleanness through the lusts of their own hearts, to dishonour their own bodies between themselves: [25] Who changed the truth of God into a lie, and worshipped and served the creature more than the Creator, who is blessed for ever. Amen.

[26] For this cause God gave them up unto vile affections: for even their women did change the natural use into that which is against nature: [27] And likewise also the men, leaving the natural use of the woman, burned in their lust one toward another; men with men working that which is unseemly, and receiving in themselves that recompence of their error which was meet.

[28] And even as they did not like to retain God in their knowledge, God gave them over to a reprobate mind, to do those things which are not convenient; [29] Being filled with all unrighteousness, fornication, wickedness, covetousness, maliciousness; full of envy, murder, debate, deceit, malignity; whisperers, [30] Backbiters, haters of God, despiteful, proud, boasters, inventors of evil things, disobedient to parents, [31] Without understanding, covenantbreakers, without natural affection, implacable, unmerciful: [32] Who knowing the judgment of God, that

they which commit such things are worthy of death, not
only do the same, but have pleasure in them that do them.

It clearly states that sodomy is condemned, and there is no mention whatsoever of temple prostitutes, or even common prostitutes for that matter. The context doesn't even hint at such a theory here. Paul said, "God also gave them up to uncleanness," (v. 24) which can also mean "physical" or "moral impurity," according to *Strong's Concordance*. The Greek word for "dishonor" in verse 24 can also mean "shame" or "maltreat and despise"; sodomy is viewed as shameful through the scriptures. Paul also used the word *atimia*, translated as "vile," but it can also mean "infamy, disgrace"; and *pathos* could be translated as "passion" or "lust"—in this case, sinful desire. In verse 27, Paul used the Greek word *phusikos*, which can mean either "natural" or "instinctive." "Error" is translated from the Greek word *plane*. Can there be any doubt by an honest truth seeker that sodomy is sin? The grouping of women with men and men with men, performing anal sex, is unnatural and goes against one's instincts; Paul also said "that recompense of their error which was meet" (v. 27), which was God's judgment against them for their sexual sins.

The scriptures are quite clear that sodomy is sin and that people who engage in this type of behavior go against nature or, more aptly, put away their God-given instinct to be with someone of the opposite sex. As wrong as it is for a man to commit adultery by having sex with another man's wife, this activity is never described as going against nature or one's instinct, as sodomy is. Even if one were to insist that these verses somehow condemn temple prostitution, this still wouldn't change the fact that people who perform anal sex are going against what is instinctive; they are in error. This is no different from someone who believes adultery is wrong only when it's with a married temple prostitute and that sex with a married nontemple prostitute is OK. Some try to argue that Paul condemned heterosexuals pretending to be homosexuals; but as we've already seen, Romans 1:26–27 condemns heterosexual *and* homosexual sodomy, so this theory simply doesn't fit. Paul also mentioned that God punished the people who engaged in these acts against nature; whether Paul referred to sodomy with temple prostitutes isn't really important—what *is* important is that sodomy is a sin. Any argument that insists these verses condemn only idolatrous sodomy is moot because sodomy still goes against nature, much like nonidolatrous bestiality.

The truth is that sodomy is a choice, whether the person engages in heterosexual or homosexual sodomy; it's simply a choice for a particular sex act. This choice is no different for the kleptomaniac, pyromaniac, alcoholic, and so forth. God expects all Christians to have temperance and not to act on sinful desires. Liken it to a worker who gets angry at his boss, exercises self-control, and doesn't hit him; so it should be for people tempted to engage in sodomy.

Sexual behavior is a choice. Anyone who denies this must admit that rapists don't have a choice when they rape someone. More to the point, those who date choose whom they want to be with, and anyone who engages in sex, unless he or she is raped, chooses whom to have sex with and the type of sex to have (anal or vaginal). Bisexuality throws a wrench into the theory of being born with a fixed sexual orientation, so homosexual proponents are left with the belief that some people choose and some don't.

Let's return to the subject of homosexual sodomy; some proponents state that the Hebrew word *toebch*, which is translated "abomination" in Leviticus 18:22 and 20:13, refers only to someone being ritually impure. The problem is that the same word is used for sins of bestiality, child sacrifice, and adultery, among other sins—all of which carried the death penalty. No comparison can be made to being clean or unclean in terms of touching certain objects, so having mixed fabrics and shaving the sides of one's head don't compare with the preceding sexual sins. God also indicated that these sexual laws were not just for the tribe of Levi but for the whole of Israel—even the strangers among them (Lev. 18:26).

The story of Sodom and Gomorrah has always gotten people's attention, especially with the growing acceptance of sodomy in Christianity. Proponents of homosexual sodomy are quick to point out that Sodom's sins were greed and the oppression of the poor (Ezek. 16:49–50). In verse 50, God even mentions they committed abomination before him. What was this abomination? But these weren't Sodom's only sins. Genesis 19:4–11 says,

> But before they lay down, the men of the city, even the men of Sodom, compassed the house round, both old and young, all the people from every quarter: And they called unto Lot, and said unto him, Where are the men which came in to thee this night? bring them out unto us, that we may know [*yada*] them. And Lot went out at the door unto them, and shut the door after him, And said, I pray you, brethren, do not so wickedly. Behold now, I have two daughters which have not known man; let me, I pray you, bring them out unto you, and do ye to them as is good in your eyes: only unto these men do nothing; for therefore came they under the shadow of my roof. And they said, Stand back. And they said again, This one fellow came in to sojourn, and he will needs be a judge: now will we deal worse with thee, than with them. And they pressed sore upon the man, even Lot, and came near to break the door. But the men put forth their hand, and pulled Lot into the house to them, and shut to the door. And they smote the men that were at the door of the house with blindness, both small and great: so that they wearied themselves to find the door.

Some have speculated that the Sodomites didn't desire to have sex with the two men (angels); they wanted only to interrogate them. The Hebrew word *yada* is translated "know," which could mean to know someone in a nonsexual way. However, the context points to *yada* in the sexual sense because Lot offered his daughters as a substitute for the angels and told the mob they were virgins. Sodomy proponents incorrectly point out that Sodom was destroyed because of the attempted gang rape of the two angels. They ignore the fact that God had already decided to destroy the city of Sodom (Gen. 18:19–20). The men who wanted to rape God's angels were already engaging in homosexual sex, whether it was consensual sex or rape. But does anyone really think all the heterosexual and homosexual anal sex taking place in Sodom was rape?

Common sense dictates that if homosexual rape was going on in Sodom, more than likely consensual homosexual sex was probably prevalent too. Is this not the judgment for sodomy God later spoke to the Israelites about, the sin that defiled the land (Lev. 18:27)? Proponents of sodomy have been able to make gains among Christians because Deuteronomy 23:17 translates *qadeshah* as "prostitute" or "whore," and *qadesh* means "sodomite" or "homosexual" in most Bible versions. The correct translation should be female and male sacred prostitutes: *qadesh* (Deut. 23:17; 1 Kings 14:24; 15:22; 22:46; 23:7; Job 36:14) and *qdeshah* (Gen. 38:21–22; Deut. 23:17; Hos. 4:14).

The fact that "sodomites" is incorrectly translated from *qadesh* instead of temple prostitute doesn't change the fact that sodomy carried the death penalty and that God forbade it in Leviticus 18:22 and 20:13. Even though God didn't have to repeat himself, the New Testament mentions and condemns sodomy. As Paul stated, "They [the ungodly and unrighteous] are without excuse" (Rom. 1:20). "And likewise also the men, leaving the natural use of the woman, burned in their lust one toward another; men with men working that which is unseemly" (Rom. 1:27). It must be emphasized again the Greek word for "use" in Romans 1:26 and 27 literally means sexual intercourse; this is further proof from God, speaking through Paul, that people aren't born homosexual. Even if God were completely silent on the issue of homosexuality, common sense should dictate that he created them male and female, not male and male. Women were created to be a suitable helper for man; any animal or another male doesn't qualify. Many people find bestiality disgusting and correctly point out that each living creature should be after its own kind, yet some of these same people believe men can have sex with men.

First Samuel 20:41 says, "And as soon as the lad was gone, David arose out of a place toward the south, and fell on his face to the ground, and bowed himself three times: and they kissed one another, and wept one with another, until David exceeded." Ironically, some proponents of sodomy reject the plain reading of Leviticus 18:22 and 20:13, yet they have no problem inferring that David and Jonathan were homosexuals. Second Samuel 1:25–26 says, "How are the mighty fallen in the midst of the battle! O Jonathan, thou wast slain in thine high places. I am distressed for thee, my brother Jonathan: very pleasant hast thou been unto me: thy love to me was wonderful, passing the love of women." David mourned the death of his friend Jonathan; any other interpretation is inferring from silence and is without merit. During this time people routinely greeted each other with a kiss—men still practice this greeting in different cultures around the world. The reality is that proponents of sodomy have nothing biblically solid to stand on, so they rely on a myriad of assumptions. They insist there is no verse that explicitly condemns sodomy, no matter how obvious it is. Then they turn around and infer that Jonathan and David, a man who had eight wives and ten concubines, were sodomites.

Their reasoning is never consistent. If sodomy isn't a sin, as they claim, then why is there not one case of a godly man lying sexually (*shakab*) with another man? They also make ridiculous claims that cannot be backed up with any solid evidence, such as "Egypt was raping the men, and this is what God was condemning in Leviticus" or "The Canaanites were practicing homosexual temple prostitution, and this is why God forbade sodomy in Leviticus." There is zero evidence that the Egyptian army was raping Hebrew male slaves, and there's also no evidence of rampant homosexual temple prostitution in Canaan.

In their continuing attempt to rewrite history, sodomites who profess the faith and their allies state that the eunuchs mentioned in the Bible were homosexuals in some or all cases. The Hebrew word for "eunuch" is *cariye* or *carie*, which literally means "to castrate." It can also refer to a minister of state. It's possible that a man could have been both a eunuch and a minister of state, but nothing in the scriptures suggests anything about someone being a homosexual; this is just a presupposition. Potiphar is an example of a man who was a minister of state, but he wasn't castrated because he had a wife; in cases where a man was called a eunuch and was in charge of a king's royal harem, he was without a doubt a man who had been castrated. An argument some proponents put forward is that these men weren't castrated but were, in fact, homosexuals put in place to protect or watch over a harem, queen, or the king's daughter.

This idea is absurd because few civilizations embraced sodomy. But even if an ancient society did, would they really take a man at his word and let him watch over women? There would have been plenty of men, professing homosexuals, who watched over the king's daughter for a long journey or looked after the queen if the king was away, they say. Such an idea is beyond ridiculous; only after a man had been castrated could he be put in charge of this task—and only then could the king trust him. Of course, any castrated man isn't going to desire a man, woman, or beast for that matter. The reality is that any biblical argument for sodomy comes up limp wristed.

As we have already seen, a plain reading of scripture showed us that Potiphar wasn't castrated because he had a wife; a similar approach to scripture tells us that Shaashgaz, the chamberlain, was a castrated man because he kept the concubines (Esther 2:14). The word for "eunuch"—in Greek, *eunouchos*—has the same definition as the Hebrew equivalent. Acts 8:27 says, "And he arose and went: and, behold, a man of Ethiopia, an eunuch of great authority under Candace queen of the Ethiopians, who had the charge of all her treasure, and had come to Jerusalem for to worship." A man such as this, who had great authority under the queen and was in charge of all her wealth, would certainly have been a castrated man. No kingdom would have placed so much authority in a man who was also close to the queen without castrating him first. Homosexual proponents believe the Ethiopian eunuch was a homosexual, but once again no kingdom would have taken someone working close to the queen at his or her word (assuming that the kingdom was tolerant of homosexuality) and would have castrated him regardless of his sexual preference.

When Jesus spoke of some eunuchs being "born from their mother's womb" (Matt. 19:12), he referred to men who were born with physical deformities that prevented them from having offspring, thus making them physical eunuchs from birth. Jesus wasn't talking about people who chose to be sodomites, and Paul would state later in Romans 1:26–27 that sodomites choose to go against nature and their God-given instinct. So when we compare scripture and remove the presupposition that eunuchs were sodomites, we are left with no choice except to say that eunuchs weren't sodomites. Why would anyone make an argument that eunuchs are men who don't have sex with women but can include men who have sex with other men?

First Corinthians 6:9 says, "Know ye not that the unrighteous shall not inherit the kingdom of God? Be not deceived: neither fornicators [*pornos*], nor idolaters, nor adulterers, nor effeminate [*malakos*], nor abusers of themselves with mankind [*asenokoites*]." Paul listed a plethora of sins that prevent people from entering into the kingdom of God. One of the terms he used, *malakos*, is translated as "effeminate," which literally means "soft to the touch." It is used to describe John the Baptist's clothes (as soft) in Matthew 11:8 and Luke 7:25. In 1 Corinthians 6:9, it is used to describe a person, not clothing. So what could the Bible mean when it describes a man as being "soft to the touch"? There are some who say *malakos* refers to cross-dressers, not homosexual sodomy in general.

Deuteronomy 22:5 says, "The woman shall not wear that which pertaineth unto a man, neither shall a man put on a woman's garment: for all that do so are abomination unto the Lord thy God." While God didn't like men and women cross-dressing, they weren't put to death; neither were they required to sacrifice an animal. Cross-dressing doesn't violate any of the fruit of the Spirit. God didn't even call cross-dressers unclean; they could have gone to the temple and left unharmed. Cross-dressing, like wearing mixed fabrics, was never a sin, so this could be ruled out as a definition of *malakos*. Another popular explanation is that *malakos* referred to men with long hair; this theory also runs into problems because in Leviticus 19:27, God says, "Ye shall not round the corners of your heads, neither shalt thou mar the corners of thy beard." Here God commanded the men of Israel not to shave their facial hair or cut the sides of their hair, meaning it would grow rather long. The Nazarite vow is more proof that having long hair isn't sin for a man.

Numbers 6:5 says, "All the days of the vow of his separation there shall no rasor come upon his head: until the days be fulfilled, in the which he separateth himself unto the Lord, he shall be holy, and shall let the locks of the hair of his head grow." We see that a man can be holy and have long hair, when we consider that a man could make a vow for years—he had long hair, yet God considered him holy.

First Corinthians 11:14 says, "Doth not even nature itself teach you, that, if a man have long hair, it is a shame unto him?" Here Paul appealed to nature on the subject of men having long hair, but note that having long hair isn't a sin. It was never a sin in the Old Testament, so it cannot be a sin in the New Testament.

By comparison sodomy isn't natural, and God commanded sodomites to be put to death. This rules out *malakos* being men with long hair, but what about some proponents' argument that *malakos* means eating and drinking? Romans 14:17–21 says,

> For the kingdom of God is not meat and drink; but righteousness, and peace, and joy in the Holy Ghost. For he that in these things serveth Christ is acceptable to God, and approved of men. Let us therefore follow after the things which make for peace, and things wherewith one may edify another. For meat destroy not the work of God. All things indeed are pure; but it is evil for that man who eateth with offence. It is good neither to eat flesh, nor to drink wine, nor any thing whereby thy brother stumbleth, or is offended, or is made weak [*astheneo*].

Malakos can't be used to describe what people eat or drink, and Paul used the Greek word *astheneo*, which means weak or feeble, not *malakos*. In summary, the word *malakos* couldn't refer to cross-dressing, men growing long hair, or eating and drinking certain foods. Could *malakos* refer to men who engage in sex with other men and play the role of a woman? This seems to be the case given the fact that Paul followed *malakos* with "abusers of themselves with mankind." This would mean that the *malakos* (or "soft ones") play the feminine or passive role, while the "abusers of themselves with mankind," or *arsenokoites*, are the active participants. Some Bible versions translate *malakos* as "catamite," which is a boy who has sex with a man. Either definition is a condemnation of homosexual sodomy. The other Greek word under contention is *arsenokoites*, which reinforces this interpretation. Paul probably created the Greek word *arsenokoites*. It comprises two different words: *arsenos*, which means "male," and *koites*, which is translated "bed." Paul literally said "male bed." What, then, did Paul mean by the term "male bed"? Many who support the sodomy argument lead people down a dead end; to justify their opinion they quote secular works with the word *arsenokoites* written centuries after Paul, or they simply say the word doesn't mean what it literally says. Rather than taking that fallacious approach, we will look at the following facts:

1. Paul spoke and wrote in Greek.
2. Most Christians throughout history have used the Septuagint.
3. The New Testament must be interpreted in light of the Old Testament.

Whenever the New Testament quotes the Old Testament, the vast majority of the time it quotes the Septuagint, which was widely used by early Christians. Paul quotes the prohibitions God gave to the Israelites. Leviticus 20:13 says, "*[K]ai hos an koimethe meta arsenos koiten gunaikos.*"

An honest reading of scripture would lead one to believe Paul condemned sodomy with the word *arsenokoites* and alluded to the ban on sodomy in Leviticus, which is still in effect. Any study of scripture must be done in light of the Old Testament; sodomy was condemned then, and it is condemned now. Some argue that you cannot always take a compound word and separate it into two individual words to get the meaning of the compound word. While this is true and an important factor to take into account, we should realize that sometimes we can define a compound word by defining each individual word.

Taking an ultraliteral approach, some proponents of sodomy state that Paul condemned only a male in a bed. A little common sense easily refutes this claim. Paul said these people won't inherit the kingdom of God; there's no way he could have been referring to a man simply lying in bed. In Romans 13:13, Paul mentioned a list of sins of the flesh, one of which is *koite*, which means "bed." Was Paul condemning all men, women, and children for simply lying in bed? No. He himself slept in bed as other single people do. Paul used *koite* to describe illicit sex or debauchery in 1 Corinthians 6:9. Paul used *arsenokoites* to denote sexual sin in—in this case—a male bed. He couldn't have referred to a man and woman engaged in illicit sexual behavior because he described this as a male bed, not just a bed, as he did in Romans 13:13. The obvious conclusion is that Paul was talking about a man having sex with another man, which would make this not only a *koites* (bed) but also an *arsenokoites* (male bed).

If God gave a command and said, "Don't eat a burger with cheese," years later Paul coined a new term and said, "Don't eat a cheeseburger." Would anybody really try to say we don't know what Paul meant when he invented the term "cheeseburger"? Does anybody think cheeseburger could refer to anything, or do we just not know what he was referring to? The common sense approach is to read what Paul said in light of what God said earlier about eating burgers with or without cheese. For an honest student of the scriptures, there's no way around it. *Arsenokoites*, or male bed, refers to sodomy. God said it in Leviticus, and Paul later emphasized it in 1 Corinthians 6:9 and 1 Timothy 1:10.

If one were to insist that *malakos* refers only to men who have sex with boys, or pederasty, *arsenokoites* still condemns sex between two consenting men, making the case against homosexual sodomy airtight. The book of Jude details the sin of Sodom and Gomorrah and compares the fallen angels' sin of going after earthly women to the homosexuality of Sodom. Jude 1:6–7 says,

> [6] And the angels which kept not their first estate, but left their own habitation, he hath reserved in everlasting chains under

darkness unto the judgment of the great day. [7] Even as Sodom and Gomorrah, and the cities about them in like manner, giving themselves over to fornication, and going after strange flesh [*heteros*], are set forth for an example, suffering the vengeance of eternal fire.

Just as angels came to earth and went after strange, or *heteros*, flesh by having sex with earthly women, so did Sodom and Gomorrah go after *heteros*, translated "strange flesh" or homosexual or heterosexual sodomy. This is where many homosexual proponents resort to blatant lies when they claim *heteros* implies that the sin of Sodom was exclusively heterosexual in nature. The Greeks had no word for "homosexual" in the early centuries when the New Testament was written. The Greek word *homos* means "same" but wasn't used to refer to what we now call homosexuals; neither was *heteros* used to denote heterosexuals. *Heteros* in Greek means "another" or "strange"; there's nothing strange about a man having sex with a woman; however, a heavenly angel going after earthly women would be considered strange flesh (v. 6), because angels and humans are different kinds of creatures.

Likewise, a man having sex with a man (v. 7) would also qualify as strange, meaning different or unnatural; this is why Jude says "in like manner" (v. 7). Both these fallen angels and men of Sodom were going after strange flesh or flesh of a different kind. This clearly goes against God's creation order; notice that Jude uses the word *ekporneuo* in verse 7. It is translated "fornication" and used only once in the New Testament. *Ekporneuo* exemplifies an extreme form of illicit sex that is unique to fallen angels and the citizens of Sodom. *The Weymouth New Testament* translates *ekporneuo* as "gross fornication," and the Concordant Translation translates it as "ultra prostitution."[3] What Jude describes isn't your typical sexual sins, such as adultery or incest, but a corruption of God's created order—heavenly angels with earthly women and men with men. These were special cases of illicit sex in which God chained the fallen angels, flooded the world, and killed everyone save Noah and his family. Sodom and Gomorrah, except Lot and his family, were completely destroyed primarily for the act of sodomy; this is why Jude uses the word *ekporneuo*, and God destroyed the inhabitants. One cannot make the case for being inhospitable, which many nations have been throughout history. The word "homosexual" wasn't used in the English language until the late nineteenth century; most early English Bibles used the word "sodomite" instead, seeing the obvious connection with the sin of Sodom.

The fact that the word "homosexual" didn't make its way into the Bible until the twentieth century is irrelevant because there was no English word to describe this behavior prior to then. The theory that these words were translated with the intent to condemn sodomy when God originally didn't is without merit. The scribes knew it referred to men having sex with men; the prohibitions in Leviticus couldn't be any clearer, and the fact that the term "homosexual" wasn't yet invented doesn't help the argument of proponents.

CHAPTER 6

Menstruation

LEVITICUS 15:19–24 SAYS,

> And if a woman have an issue, and her issue in her flesh be blood, she shall be put apart seven days: and whosoever toucheth her shall be unclean until the even. And every thing that she lieth upon in her separation shall be unclean: every thing also that she sitteth upon shall be unclean. And whosoever toucheth her bed shall wash his clothes, and bathe himself in water, and be unclean until the even. And whosoever toucheth any thing that she sat upon shall wash his clothes, and bathe himself in water, and be unclean until the even. And if it be on her bed, or on any thing whereon she sitteth, when he toucheth it, he shall be unclean until the even. And if any man lie with her at all, and her flowers be upon him, he shall be unclean seven days; and all the bed whereon he lieth shall be unclean.

These verses deal with a woman who, during her period, is unclean for seven days. Anything she touches is unclean for the day, including the man who touches the bed she lies in. If he lies in bed with her and comes in contact with her blood, he is unclean for seven days (v. 24).

These and other cleanliness laws were put in place only because of God's physical tabernacle. Since God no longer dwells in a temple made with hands (Acts 7:48) and will never dwell in one again, these laws of cleanliness are no longer in effect. Jesus was baptized and cleansed for our good (Matt. 3:14–15), and his righteousness has been imputed to us (2 Cor. 5:21). Further, God has written his laws on our hearts (Jer. 31:33; Heb. 10:16); he dwells in us because our bodies are his temple (1 Cor. 3:16). It's not that the law has been abolished because Jesus didn't come to abolish the law; it's just that his life has rendered parts of it obsolete.

Leviticus 18:19 says, "Also thou shalt not approach unto a woman to uncover her nakedness, as long as she is put apart for her uncleanness." This verse is mentioned in between incest (v. 18) and adultery (v. 20). God actually mentions sex during menstruation more than he does bestiality, yet so many Christians choose to ignore this point.

> Defile not ye yourselves in any of these things: for in all these the nations are defiled which I cast out before you: And the land is defiled: therefore I do visit the iniquity thereof upon it, and the land itself vomiteth out her inhabitants. Ye shall therefore keep my statutes and my judgments, and shall not commit any of these abominations; neither any of your own nation, nor any stranger that sojourneth among you: (For all these abominations have the men of the land done, which were before you, and the land is defiled;) That the land spue not you out also, when ye defile it, as it spued out the nations that were before you. For whosoever shall commit any of these abominations, even the souls that commit them shall be cut off from among their people. Therefore shall ye keep mine ordinance, that ye commit not any one of these abominable customs, which were committed before you, and that ye defile not yourselves therein: I am the Lord your God. (Lev. 18:24–30)

> And if a man shall lie with a woman having her sickness, and shall uncover her nakedness; he hath discovered her fountain, and she hath uncovered the fountain of her blood: and both of them shall be cut off from among their people. (Lev. 20:18)

One could surmise that sex during menstruation involved God killing the participants of such a practice himself, similar to the death of Onan mentioned earlier. Second Samuel 11:4 says, "And David sent messengers, and took her; and she came in unto him, and he lay with her; for she was purified from her uncleanness: and she returned unto her house."

David had no problem committing adultery with Uriah's wife Bathsheba, but he made sure she was no longer having her period when he had sex with her. God required that there be two witnesses to witness a crime worthy of death. David made sure there were no witnesses, and he made sure she was no longer having her period. This seems to lend credence to the fact that sex during menstruation could have involved God directly killing the practitioners. Since Bathsheba had just had her period, there was no way the child would be Uriah's; this is why David was so adamant for Uriah to have sex with his wife (2 Sam. 11:8, 13).

God gave readers his view on menstruating women. It is the duty of those who wish to be blameless to obey his laws.

> But if a man be just, and do that which is lawful and right, And hath not eaten upon the mountains, neither hath lifted up his eyes to the idols of the house of Israel, neither hath defiled his neighbour's wife, neither hath come near to a menstruous woman. (Ezek. 18:5–6)

> In thee are men that carry tales to shed blood: and in thee they eat upon the mountains: in the midst of thee they commit lewdness. In thee have they discovered their fathers' nakedness: in thee have they humbled her that was set apart for pollution. (Ezek. 22:9–10)

What does God compare menstruation to?

> Son of man, when the house of Israel dwelt in their own land, they defiled it by their own way and by their doings: their way was before me as the uncleanness of a removed woman. (Ezek. 36:17)

> Ye shall defile also the covering of thy graven images of silver, and the ornament of thy molten images of gold: thou shalt cast them away as a menstruous cloth; thou shalt say unto it, Get thee hence. (Isa. 30:22)

> But we are all as an unclean thing, and all our righteousnesses are as filthy [*ed*] rags. (Isa. 64:6)

The Hebrew word for "filthy" in this famous verse, which is *ed*, refers to menstrual flux. "Our righteousness is like a woman's menstrual rags" would be a more accurate translation of this verse.

What God said about menses in Leviticus 15 is related to the cleanliness laws for a physical temple, which no longer exists; however, God forbade sex during this time in chapters 18 and 20. So a man is now allowed to touch anything a menstruating woman touched and could sleep in the same bed as she and still be clean, and a woman is no longer unclean. This in no way should be confused with God's forbidding sex during menstruation, as we see in chapters 18 and 20. Any couple who engages in sex while a woman is having her period is sinning.

Unfortunately, many Christians, especially apologists, conflate the issue by combining Leviticus 15 with 18 and 20, omitting the fact that chapter 15 rendered one unclean for only a period of time, whereas in chapters 18 and 20, having sex with a woman during menstruation gave the participants the death sentence. Whether they were supernatural deaths from God isn't the point; the act required death.

Further proof that separates chapters 18 and 20 as being sin versus chapter 15 is that God's blanket condemnation of sexual sins also included the heathen nations listed in Leviticus 18:24, and sex with a menstruating woman is listed right along with adultery. The same scenario holds true in Leviticus 20:23; this is proof that having sex with a woman during her period was just as much a sin as sodomy or bestiality. However, there was no blanket statement where God said the heathen nations were guilty of the cleanliness laws of Leviticus 15; this fact reinforces the conclusion that these cleanliness laws were limited only to ancient Israel.

Many Christians wonder why God condemned sex during menstruation; seemingly the reason why is somewhat similar to God's prohibition on sodomy. The fact is that the anus isn't a vagina; it isn't designed for penetration. On the other hand, the vagina *is* made for penetration, but when a woman goes through her menstrual cycle, it is during this time that her body naturally sheds the thickened uterine lining and extra blood through the vagina. During this period the vagina isn't ready for penetration, which explains why God forbade the practice; sex during this time is just as unnatural as homosexual or heterosexual sodomy. It would actually be hypocritical for God to allow sodomy but not sex during a woman's period or vice versa. Unfortunately, most Christians aren't aware of how consistent God's law is and incorrectly believe he doesn't prohibit the practice.

In summary, a couple shouldn't engage in sex while a woman is menstruating. The seven-day waiting period of Leviticus 15 doesn't have to be observed since this was related to the cleanliness laws of simply touching a menstruating woman. Note that God's prohibitions in Leviticus 18 and 20 don't have the seven-day period listed; there's only a prohibition during the time she's on her period.

CHAPTER 7

Incest, Bestiality and Customs

INCEST

In terms of incestuous unions, the Bible clearly specifies that these are forbidden. You couldn't uncover the nakedness of (have sex with) any of the following:

- Father or mother (Lev. 18:7)
- Father's wife (v. 8)
- Sister, daughter of your father or daughter of your mother born at home (v. 9)
- Son's daughter, daughter's daughter (v. 10)
- Daughter of your father's wife (v. 11)
- Sister of your father (v. 12)
- Mother's sister (v. 13)
- Father's brother and/or his wife (v. 14)
- Daughter-in-law (v. 15)
- Brother's wife (v. 16)
- Woman and her daughter, her son's daughter, or her daughter's daughter (v. 17)
- A woman and her sister while she is alive to vex [her] (v. 18)

Anyone who committed any of these acts was cut off (v. 29). Recently a plethora of books have purported to show that the scriptures regarding sex are solely about property rights but not about morality per se. They claim scripture doesn't forbid a father from having sex with his daughter, so the laws of God aren't really about morality but about property. Nothing could be further from the truth. Leviticus 18:6 says, "None of you shall approach to any that is near of kin to him, to uncover their nakedness." Who would deny that a father and daughter are near kin? They also fail to grasp Leviticus 18:17, which forbids a man from having sex with a woman and her daughter, keeping in mind that "woman" in Hebrew can also mean "wife," so this forbids not only a father and his daughter but a stepdaughter or a woman he isn't married to and her daughter. Leviticus 18:17 is, in fact, airtight in this regard; also note that if God's laws were all about property rights, why would he forbid sex with a woman during her period and anal sex? And adultery would be permitted with permission from the husband, but scripture doesn't even hint at such nonsense. Anyone who thinks that a father can have sex with his daughter simply doesn't understand scripture, which clearly forbids this and other incestuous relationships.

BESTIALITY

Bestiality is a sin that is explicitly condemned in scripture. The following scriptures speak for themselves:

> Whosoever lieth with a beast shall surely
> be put to death. (Exod. 22:19)

> Neither shalt thou lie with any beast to defile thyself
> therewith: neither shall any woman stand before a beast
> to lie down thereto: it is confusion. (Lev. 18:23)

> Cursed be he that lieth with any manner of beast. And
> all the people shall say, Amen. (Deut. 27:21)

CUSTOMS
AGE DIFFERENCES

Many Christians in the Western world are unaware that people during biblical times married when they were far younger than are people in the

West. The custom many still practice today is to marry as soon as a child hits puberty or not long afterward. In most cases a dowry must still be paid to the parents, so the husband is often several years older than his wife. This is no different from biblical times when women were given in marriage soon after their first period. Moreover, she would have been pledged to be married years before. This custom is still practiced throughout the world, regardless of race, culture, or religion.

There has been an uproar of criticism from Christians against Muslims who marry girls who are eight, ten, seven, or even six years old. What many fail to realize is that even today many Christians still marry at puberty and even collect a dowry from their virgin daughter. There wasn't anything wrong with this during biblical times, so why would it be a sin now? Daughters would be pledged to marry at a young age but continue to live with their parents until they had their first period; then they would be given away in marriage.

First Kings 1:1–4 says,

> Now king David was old and stricken in years; and they covered him with clothes, but he gat no heat. Wherefore his servants said unto him, Let there be sought for my lord the king a young virgin: and let her stand before the king, and let her cherish him, and let her lie in thy bosom, that my lord the king may get heat. So they sought for a fair damsel throughout all the coasts of Israel, and found Abishag a Shunammite, and brought her to the king. And the damsel was very fair, and cherished the king, and ministered to him: but the king knew her not.

The solution to King David's old age, according to his advisers, was to give him a virgin to keep him "warm." While it's true that David never had sex with her, this doesn't change the fact that David was significantly older than most of his wives and concubines. It's safe to say that David wasn't marrying a twenty-five-year-old virgin. He inherited some of his lovers from Saul (2 Sam. 12:8); others, however, he found for himself (1 Sam. 25: 23–42; 2 Sam. 3:3–5). Since a virgin dowry was quite expensive, it could take several years for a man to save up enough money to marry a woman. Therefore, the husband was often several years older than his wife. Jacob loved Rachel, but he had no money, so he had to work fourteen years for her (Gen. 29:27). In some circumstances, the firstborn son had to take care of his mother when his father passed away, which made it even harder and longer for him to save up enough money to get married.

In the New Testament this fact was still a reality. Mary was about to be given to Joseph in marriage; most historians believe she was twelve to fifteen years old and that she had been pledged to be his wife at an even earlier age. When the angel Gabriel told Mary she would give birth to the Messiah, she was confused because she was a virgin (Luke 1:34). Mary had the option to reject this proclamation, but she assented to God's will. "And Mary said, Behold the handmaid of the Lord; be it unto me according to thy word. And the angel departed from her" (Luke 1:38).

The previous verses refute the belief that Mary had no choice in the matter; she clearly told Gabriel, "Be it unto me according to thy word." Many Christians recoil at the thought of Mary being twelve to fifteen years old; they think that's too young. Still, when a female has her first period, it's a biological fact that she's ready for motherhood. Did it ever occur to the critics of early marriage that if God believed getting married young was wrong, he would have made female menstruation happen at a later time in life? Although "Christian" movies portray Mary as a twenty-two-year-old virgin marrying a twenty-five-year-old Joseph, the reality is strikingly different. In fact, it's unlikely she was even fifteen years old. She was probably twelve or thirteen, and Joseph was in his late twenties or early thirties. This means Mary was in her late forties when Jesus, while on the cross, asked John to take care of her. This also more than likely proves Joseph was significantly older than Mary and had already passed away (John 19:26–27).

As for pedophilia, the scriptures teach that people shouldn't engage in sex until they've gone through puberty—hence the tokens of virginity (Deut. 22:15). All prepubescent sex is rape since the body isn't biologically ready for sex. Even today a country with no age of consent, such as Saudi

Arabia, requires puberty as a minimum before someone can consummate a marriage. In many Western nations, the age of consent is fourteen or fifteen years, which is only one to two years after puberty. It's also not uncommon for Westerners who trace their lineage (you don't have to go that far back either) to find an ancestor who was married at twelve or fourteen. Scripturally speaking, any prepubescent sex is rape and is a sin; also, any type of sexual molestation is just as wrong as any type of assault.

CHAPTER 8

Sex in Heaven

IF THERE'S ONE ANSWER THAT proves most Christians are prudish regarding sex, it's their response when asked about whether there will be sex in the new heaven and earth. Most respond with an emphatic no. When we study scripture, however, the evidence that sex will continue to exist is quite overwhelming.

Genesis 1:28 says, "And God blessed them and God said unto them be fruitful and multiply and replenish the earth." This important verse proves a critical point—that sex was created before the fall when sin and death entered mankind. From the very beginning, if Adam hadn't sinned, man would have lived forever and walked with God, and sex would have still been part of life. Sex isn't something God created as a result of sin and death entering the world. If God had given Adam and Eve reproductive capabilities to propagate the human race *after* the fall, then the onus would have been on the author to prove that sex continues in the new heavens and earth. However, this isn't the case. Sex and sexual desire were created before the fall, not after it.

Genesis 1:31 says, "And God saw everything that he had made [including sex] and behold it was very good." The burden of proof is actually on those who believe sex is temporary and will no longer exist when all things are restored with a new heaven and earth (Acts 3:21; Rev. 21:1). The antisex proponents sometimes refer to Genesis 4:1, where the scriptures state that Eve conceived Cain after the fall, so they conclude that sex didn't exist until after Adam and Eve were cursed. This conclusion ignores Genesis 1:28, where God told them to be fruitful and multiply before the fall.

The other problem they have is that man was made in the image of God. When the scriptures speak of the image of God, they refer to the attributes of God: love, patience, wisdom, forgiveness, and the ability to create life because men and women procreate through sex. Here are three positions that characterize the prevailing Christian view on sex in heaven:

1. God created sex so men and women could procreate, because death and sin entered the world. This position ignores Genesis 1:28; more importantly, scripture doesn't state or even hint that this view is correct. They also have man gaining an attribute of God, the ability to create life through procreation as a result of sin.
2. Some believe sex existed before the fall, but it will no longer be needed when creation is restored and we live in a new heaven and earth (Acts 3:21; Rev. 21:1). They run into a similar problem; man would actually be regressing with his relationship with God. In this scenario man would have originally had the procreative attribute of God before the fall. He would keep this attribute during the fall but lose it when he is restored with a new body (Phil. 3:20–21). But is man really restored if he loses an attribute he originally possessed?
3. The only scriptural solution is that man was created in the image of God before the fall, and this included the ability to procreate. This attribute stayed with man after the fall, and it will be with him when he is restored.

Not only is the view that sex was created solely to propagate the human race not scriptural; it also ignores the fact that God gave us the ability to have an orgasm while having sex purely for the purpose of pleasure, when he, in fact, didn't have to do so. How many Christians who hold this view have sex only for procreation and stop having sex once they're finished having children? Sex is part of our nature; it's one of the many attributes that makes us human. If sex were only for procreation, why does the desire for it still exist when people are sterile or past the age to reproduce? The desire might decrease as we get older, but it's still there.

The most common scriptural evidence that there will be no sex in heaven is Matthew 22:30. "For in the resurrection they neither marry nor are given in marriage, but are as the angels of God in heaven." Most Christians who use this verse as proof ignore that the question asked of Jesus was about marriage, not about sex (Matt. 22:24–28). The Saducees didn't ask him whether there would be any sex in heaven or whether we would be sexless. Jesus said only that there would be no marriage in heaven, yet people continue to take this verse out of context and say sex will no longer exist, or that we will be genderless like angels. Not only are angels not sexless, as we will later see, but they offer further proof that sex is part of being human and will still exist in heaven. Going back to the Old Testament we read that

> He that is wounded in the stones or hath his privy member cut off, shall not enter into the congregation of the Lord. (Deut. 23:1)

> And the Lord spake unto Moses, saying, Speak unto Aaron, saying, Whosoever he be of thy seed in their generations that hath any blemish, let him not approach to offer the bread of his God. For whatsoever man he be that hath a blemish, he shall not approach: a blind man, or a lame, or he that hath a flat nose, or any thing superfluous. Or a man that is brokenfooted, or brokenhanded, Or crookbackt, or a dwarf, or that hath a blemish in his eye, or be scurvy, or scabbed, or hath his stones broken; No man that hath a blemish of the seed of Aaron the priest shall come nigh to offer the offerings of the Lord made by fire: he hath a blemish; he shall not come nigh to offer the bread of his God. He shall eat the bread of his God, both of the most holy, and of the holy. Only he shall not go in unto the vail, nor come nigh unto the altar, because he hath a blemish; that he profane not my sanctuaries: for

I the Lord do sanctify them. And Moses told it unto Aaron, and
to his sons, and unto all the children of Israel. (Lev. 21:16–24)

But why did God make such prohibitions against men who had defects regardless of whether they were born that way or not? Either of the following scenarios can be true:

1. God said that people who have these defects are sinners as a result of their disabilities. While it is true that blindness and leprosy are types of sins in the Bible, how does this explain men who have their male organs cut off? Or have no privy members? Or even dwarfs, for that matter? Jesus said some were eunuchs for the kingdom's sake (Matt. 19:12). Does anybody seriously believe going without sex is a type of sin?
2. One could argue that the blind, eunuchs, dwarfs, and so forth weren't allowed, but this was only for ancient Israel. While this is true, we must remember that the Old Testament was filled with types and shadows, so these prohibitions must exist for a reason. But what is it? It would seem that these laws against defects, whether they were the result of man's actions or through birth, resulting in being prohibited from entering God's congregation or assembly, are a shadow of the consummation of God's kingdom when everyone will have immortal, unblemished, glorified bodies without physical defects.

God's prohibition on men suffering crushed or missing testicles and being dwarfs is a foreshadowing of the resurrection when everyone will have immortal, ageless, perfect bodies. There won't be any dwarfs or men with missing testicles, crooked backs, blindness, deafness, and so forth. Yes, blind men will be able to see, and men born as eunuchs (or made to be so) will be made whole. Of course, it's safe to conclude that if a eunuch is made whole, he and everyone else will have a sex drive too.

Isaiah 56:4–5 says,

> For thus saith the Lord unto the eunuchs that keep my sabbaths, and choose the things that please me, and take hold of my covenant; Even unto them will I give in mine house and within my walls a place and a name better than of sons and of daughters: I will give them an everlasting name, that shall not be cut off.

This is further proof that God has nothing against anyone's defects and that when we're all raised, our bodies will be perfect. These rules against defects and against the Levites are a foreshadowing of all believers being members of God's priesthood (1 Pet. 2:19) without any sin, defect, scars, or blemishes. Deuteronomy 23:1 referred to all men, not just the priests. Unlike the defects mentioned in Leviticus, also note that it doesn't matter whether they were intentional, accidental, or through birth. Men who were eunuchs weren't allowed in God's assembly.

The traditional teachings of most Christians have Jesus marrying the *ecclesia* for eternity and having spiritual intercourse, but with men and women either being sexless or having sexual organs and no sex drive, none of these teachings make sense. The spiritual/physical duality is ignored. How can there be spiritual unity between Christ and the *ecclesia* but none between men and women? So we will be one in spirit with Christ, even as he is one with the Father, but men and women won't be one physically ever again? One must ask the obvious question: Why did God even give us bodies? Shouldn't we just be floating spirits forever? Why would he give us bodies in the resurrection if we won't be able to enjoy the things we can do now with them? Wouldn't it make more sense for us to have even more enjoyment with them than we do now? We will have bodies and be able to eat, drink, and play sports, but we apparently won't be able to engage in sex. We have already seen that sex outside of marriage isn't a sin, so the idea that sex won't exist in heaven because there will no longer be marriage is false. Marriage is defined by death, but in the resurrection we will all be made immortal; marriage between men and women will no longer be necessary because we will never die.

Since God instituted marriage to be for life, when those who are dead are raised from the dead and those who are still alive are made immortal, we will be released from our marriage vows. The fact that everyone will be released from his or her marriage vow doesn't mean people who were alive and married during past ages can't have sex together in heaven. Does anyone really believe God would stop Adam and Eve from reuniting? With marriage ceasing to exist in the kingdom of God, this would mean that no one will belong exclusively to one person. But this doesn't mean that sexual relationships won't exist.

There won't be any more sin, so no one will take advantage of anybody; neither jealousy nor envy will be present. We need to keep in mind that marriage is until death. It's important to understand that Israel is married to God and that Jesus is married to the *ecclesia*. These marriages will last forever because God cannot and won't die. Though Jesus died, he wasn't betrothed to the *ecclesia* until after he rose from the dead and was made immortal. Scripturally, both of the marriages to God and Jesus are valid even in the postresurrection world because there's only one God and one Messiah. There will never be any other. On the other hand, marriages between men and women won't be allowed because we will never die, and there will be innumerable men and women. To place limits on these possibilities for eternity in a sinless universe would be odd, to say the least.

During the forty days Jesus walked the earth after his resurrection, he demonstrated that he still had a physical body that had the same functions and anatomy it did before he died. So we can say Jesus's body still had a digestive system, as he proved when he ate fish and a honeycomb (Luke 24: 41–43). In addition, he still had a brain and a heart, and we must conclude he had blood in his resurrected body. Many believe that Jesus's stating he had a body of flesh and bone means we won't have blood. However, if you believe Jesus's body rose from the dead and left the tomb, it's hard to argue that his anatomy changed.

Remember, when God created man, he said his creation was good; there was nothing wrong with the flesh-and-blood body God had given Adam, but God cursed it when he sinned. God placed the curse on Adam and all his descendants, who are under the curse of death, meaning that our bodies are perishable, corrupted by sin. But because of Jesus's victory over death, our bodies, which God himself said were anatomically good, will be restored and will be incorruptible, imperishable, and spiritual.

This is the context in which Paul wrote 1 Corinthians 15:42–44.

> So also is the resurrection of the dead. It is sown in corruption; it is raised in incorruption: It is sown in dishonour; it is raised in glory: it is sown in weakness; it is raised in power: It is sown a natural body; it is raised a spiritual body. There is a natural body, and there is a spiritual body. And so it is written, The first man Adam was made a living soul; the last Adam was made a quickening spirit. Howbeit that was not first which is spiritual, but that which is natural; and afterward that which is spiritual. The first man is of the earth, earthy: the second man is the Lord from heaven. As is the earthy, such are they also that are earthy: and as is the heavenly, such are they also that are heavenly. And as we have borne the image of the earthy, we shall also bear the image of the heavenly. Now this I say, brethren, that flesh and blood cannot inherit the kingdom of God; neither doth corruption inherit incorruption. Behold, I shew you a mystery; We shall not all sleep, but we shall all be changed, In a moment, in the twinkling of an eye, at the last trump: for the trumpet shall sound, and the dead shall be raised incorruptible, and we shall be changed. For this corruptible must put on incorruption, and this mortal must put on immortality. So when this corruptible shall have put on incorruption, and this mortal shall have put on immortality, then shall be brought to pass the saying that is written, Death is swallowed up in victory.

If we are changed when we are resurrected from the dead or when we are alive at the Second Coming, our anatomy won't be. We must be changed because of the curse God placed on us as the result of sin. Our current cursed bodies of flesh and blood cannot inherit God's kingdom, but our glorified flesh-and-blood bodies can. When Paul spoke of a spiritual (v. 44) body, he didn't mean we will be floating spirits—to take Paul literally would be an oxymoron because you cannot have an invisible corporeal body. When he spoke of a spiritual body, he was talking only in terms of a body that can inherit God's kingdom, which will still contain a physical or material, corporeal universe.

Our bodies will also be scar-free. Some Christians believe we will keep our scars because Jesus showed Thomas the holes in his hands and the scar in his wounded side. He did this to prove who he was because when he first appeared to his disciples after his resurrection, they didn't recognize him (Luke 24:15–30). It's hard to believe Jesus could spend so much time with his disciples, and they couldn't recognize the holes in his wrists and the scars on his face. More than likely, Jesus had the ability to show his scars from the crucifixion, and he appeared to them without showing them at first. He later showed them to Thomas to prove who he was. We should remember that he had scars all over his body; his back was whipped, his face was beaten, and he had a crown of thorns on his head. Yet Christians believe he kept these scars when he appeared with his disciples; that they didn't recognize him with the scars on his head from the crown of thorns and bruises on his face is absurd.

John 20:19 states that he suddenly appeared in a locked room; it doesn't say he walked through the door like a ghost. Jesus's body didn't see decay (Acts 2:31); he rose to life in the same body he was crucified in, which means he still had blood in his body. His anatomy was the same, but he had the ability to do certain deeds, such as appear at will, which he apparently couldn't have done before. Some Christians believe blood is inherently evil, but if this is the case, why were we purchased by the blood of Jesus (1 Pet. 1:18–19)? His blood was also innocent (Acts 20:28). Why would this be the case if blood were evil?

Jesus's body was innocent because he never sinned; this also includes his flesh. Fallen man, on the other hand, has been cursed, so our flesh and blood are corrupted as a result of sin and God's curse. This is why we must be changed through Jesus Christ, who proves there's nothing inherently wrong or evil about the human body but that it is good just as God first declared it to be in Genesis 1:31. Procreation, which is a form of exercising dominion over the earth and God's other creations, will continue.

LIKE THE ANGELS IN HEAVEN

A common misconception among many Christians is that angels don't possess bodies; they are incorporeal, invisible spirits. But the Bible describes angels not only as having bodies but also as having a gender. Three angels met Abraham, and the Bible describes them as men (Gen. 18:1). These angels had their feet washed (v. 4), and they also ate (v. 8). This would be impossible if they were only spirits. Angels met Lot in Sodom, and once again the Bible describes them as men who ate food and were about to go to sleep before the men of the city wanted to have sex with them (Gen. 19:4).

Many people refer to Hebrews 1:14, which states, "Are they not all ministering spirits, sent forth to minister for them who shall be heirs of salvation." But the fact that the word "spirits" is used doesn't mean angels are disembodied spirits, as so many falsely believe. The previous accounts, along with numerous others, which clearly describe angels as having bodies, would have to be ignored. When Paul spoke of a spiritual body in 1 Corinthians 15:44, he didn't mean we will be disembodied spirits floating around for eternity. When he mentioned the last Adam (Jesus) in verse 45, being a quickening spirit doesn't mean Jesus was a ghost after his resurrection. He is clearly described as having a physical body.

Why, then, do so many Christians believe angels are ministering spirits that have no physical bodies? Scripture doesn't support this view. Genesis 6:4 says, "There were giants in the earth in those days; and also after that, when the sons of God came in unto the daughters of men, and they bare children to them, the same became mighty men which were of old, men of renown." Charles Lee Brenton's Septuagint has "angels of God" in its footnotes as a possible substitution for "sons of God."[4]

The book of Job also illuminates the fact that the "sons of God" were celestial beings. Job 1:6 says, "Now there was a day when the sons of God came to present themselves before the Lord, and Satan came also among them." The adversary or Satan is a celestial being and was among the other angels who stood before God when God gave Satan permission to test Job. We also know from Job 38:7 that the angels were present during the creation of the earth.

The context of Genesis 6:4 shows that the phrase "sons of God" refers to angels and "giants." It is translated from the Hebrew word *nephilim*, which comes from the word *naphal*, which means "fall" or "to fall." The giants the Bible describes are actually fallen ones or demons; because of their lineage from heaven, they are the children of the fallen angels, who sinned by having sex with the daughters of men. The interpretation many people use to deny fallen angels had sex with earthly humans says the sons of God represent the "godly" line of Seth, who married the "ungodly" line of Cain. This reasoning has many problems. Where does the Bible state that the sons of Seth are all righteous and that the sons of Cain are all evil? The very fact that only Noah, his wife, his sons, and their wives were saved in the ark disproves the idea of the sons of Seth all being godly.

Genesis 4:26 states that when Seth's son Enos was born, men began to profane the name of the Lord. Many translations erroneously translate this as "then began men to (*chalal*) call upon the name of the Lord." The Hebrew word *chalal* means "to profane," proving that the sons of Seth were not all righteous.

The book of Enoch goes into detail about the fallen angels coming down to earth and taking wives from the daughters of men. Enoch 6:1–6 says,

> [1] And it came to pass when the children of men had multiplied that in those days were born unto them beautiful and comely daughters. [2] And the angels, the children of the heaven, saw and lusted after them, and said to one another: "Come, let us choose us wives from among the children of men and beget us children." [3] And Semjâzâ, who was their leader, said unto them: "I fear ye will not indeed agree to do this deed, and I alone shall have to pay the penalty of a great sin." [4] And they all answered him and said: "Let us all swear an oath, and all bind ourselves by mutual imprecations not to abandon this plan but to do this thing." [5] Then sware they all together and bound themselves by mutual imprecations upon it. [6] And they were in all two hundred;

who descended in the days of Jared on the summit of Mount Hermon, and they called it Mount Hermon, because they had sworn and bound themselves by mutual imprecations upon it.

From these verses come several important points. First, these angels lusted after earthly women. As we discussed earlier, "lust" simply means "desire"; however, the desire in this case is forbidden. The fact that they desired to have sex with the daughters of men is proof that angels have a sex drive. For those who believe angels don't possess bodies, this is problematic. This issue coincides with Genesis 6:4, which some avoid by saying these angels were simply spirits who possessed human bodies. But if this were the case, how could these children be men of renown? They would just be regular earthly human beings.

Spirits don't have bodies, so they cannot have sex; nor do they have sex drives. These angels would have had bodies and sex drives in order to have sex. This evidence, combined with other scriptures that describe angels eating and having their feet washed, is further proof that they aren't spirits in the literal sense.

Second, these angels knew they were committing a great sin (Enoch 6:3); the word *ekporneuo* corroborates this in Jude 1:6–7. The word means "utterly unchaste" or "ultra fornication or prostitution." Thus, angels have bodies of their own, and their decision to have sex with earthly humans was an egregious sin.

Third, many people who correctly believe angels have bodies believe there are no female angels and that women exist only on this earth. Why would God give angelic men sexual reproductive capabilities? Why would he give them a sexual desire and then forbid them from having any sex? Why would God create women on earth as companions for men and, at the same time, give angels no female companionship? And, to top it off, why give them the same sexual desires men on earth have and then punish them for having sex with earthly women?

Common sense dictates that God wouldn't give these male angels this ability without there being female angels. This would explain God's anger and severe punishment for their sin. These angels left their first estate to cohabitate with earthly women (Jude 1:6–7).

The fourth point is that this happened during the days of Jared, who was Enoch's father, which means "to descend or descent"; he was given this name because the angels descended from heaven to earth when he was born (Enoch 6:6). "Jordan" means "land of the descent," so ancient Jordan more than likely included Mount Hermon.

Remember, we read that the fallen angels taught man how to carry out an abortion. How could they teach this unless they already had experience with it? Logic would dictate that they had learned this forbidden knowledge during their first estate and taught it to men after they descended to earth.

First Corinthians 11:10 says, "For this cause ought the woman to have power on her head because of the angels." Not only does it follow that sexual desire is something the angels also possess, but Enoch also describes them several times as possessing "sexual organs" the size of horses (Enoch 88:3). Therefore, it seems that these angelic men were pretty well endowed. The reason why we covered so many scriptures dealing with angels is that Jesus said in Matthew 22:30, "For in the resurrection they neither marry, nor are given in marriage, but are as the angels of God in heaven."

Given the fact that angels were recorded as having sex and that we will be like them, it's safe to say that sex will exist in the new heavens and earth. Since God declared that his creation of man and woman was good, then we can logically expect sex to still exist. We know circumcision was a shadow of circumcision of the heart. We can also conclude that men will be uncircumcised in the resurrection because God declared everything he made was good, and that included an uncircumcised Adam. Despite what many Christian apologists say, God didn't command circumcision for health reasons, and most doctors agree it is an unnecessary procedure. Common sense should lead one to believe that a circumcised penis isn't as sensitive as one that isn't, which would lead to more sensation during sex. When God commanded the Israelites to get circumcised, it was a temporary maiming that God will restore when we are resurrected to immortality. Not only should we expect sex to be present in the resurrection to immortality, but it should also be more pleasurable than it is now.

The trap many Christians fall into regarding God's laws of sex is that they are more interested in the temporal than in the eternal, and yet patience is one of the fruits of the Spirit. We either have this fruit, or we don't. Instead of a divorced woman staying single and seeking reconciliation with her husband, she and unfortunately many professing Christians would rather disobey God's laws for selfish, temporary pleasure than obey him and be rewarded in the resurrection, even though all current earthly pleasures will still exist and be even better than they are now. Focusing on what's temporary and disobeying God will always result in pain and suffering, as King David discovered. Unfortunately, many professing Christians will discover the same fate in the lake of fire.

NOTES

1. Flavius Josephus, *The Works of Flavius Josephus*, accessed July 7, 2015, http://sacred-texts.com/jud/josephus/ant-17.htm.

2. Joseph Bryant Rotherham, *Rotherham's Emphasized Bible* (Kregel Publications, 1959), 145.

3. *Concordant Literal New Testament*, Canyon Country (Concordant Publishing Concern, 1983).

4. C. L. Brenton, *The Septuagint with Apocrypha* (Samuel Bagster & Sons, Ltd., 1851), 16.

Made in the USA
Middletown, DE
06 December 2019